Robert Hall Baynes

English Lyrics

A collection of English poetry of the present day

Robert Hall Baynes

English Lyrics
A collection of English poetry of the present day

ISBN/EAN: 9783744774833

Printed in Europe, USA, Canada, Australia, Japan

Cover: Foto ©Thomas Meinert / pixelio.de

More available books at **www.hansebooks.com**

ALL SAINTS.

English Lyrics

A

COLLECTION OF ENGLISH POETRY

OF THE PRESENT DAY.

ARRANGED BY THE

REV. ROBERT H. BAYNES, M.A.

Editor of the "Lyra Anglicana."

LONDON
HOULSTON AND WRIGHT
65, PATERNOSTER ROW
MDCCCLXV.

TO THE RIGHT REVEREND

THE LORD BISHOP OF OXFORD,

Chancellor of the Most Noble the Order of the Garter,

IN

𝔊rateful 𝔐emory of many 𝔎indnesses,

𝔚ith deep 𝔕espect and 𝔕everent 𝔄ffection,

THIS COLLECTION

OF

𝔈nglish 𝔏yrics,

WITH HIS LORDSHIP'S PERMISSION,

IS INSCRIBED.

PREFACE.

The following Collection of "English Lyrics" is intended as a companion volume to "Lyra Anglicana." The very large measure of success which attended the publication of the "Lyra" suggested the idea of the present Book, whilst it abundantly confirmed the remarks I there ventured to make as to the value of really good Hymns, and their abiding influence on the Heart and Life. And it is because I have so deep and growing a conviction of the power of this influence, that I regard it as no light privilege to have been permitted in any degree either to awaken or strengthen, in earnest and thoughtful minds, the sense of its real and practical importance.

The greatest Christian Poet of our land and age has sung to us of those who, amid toils and sorrows,—

> "Ply their daily task with busier feet,
> Because their secret souls a holy strain repeat."

And this language is no exaggeration whatsoever. There is a marvellous power of consolation and of strength about true Poetry, lighting up as it does, with its own special brightness, that which often seems to be material and commonplace, and bringing home to us, in the way easiest of all to be remembered, the great lessons God would have us learn amid the trials and discipline of our earthly life.

Most men, I suppose, who have any claim to be considered thoughtful at all, have at certain times of their history felt the force of this power of which I speak. Amid the multitudinous forms of beauty and delight in the world around; amid the shadows and the stillness when we go forth to meditate at eventide; in the darkened chamber of sickness, or in the hour of bitter sorrow, who of us does not know what it is to have his soul uplifted, comforted, or made strong, by the familiar strains of one to whom God has vouchsafed the high gift of Poetry and Song?

And in these days of hurry and excitement, when men's powers and energies are taxed to the uttermost in the various callings they pursue, and when comparatively few have time or even inclination to enter on a long and systematic study of English Poetry for themselves, it can hardly be a useless or unimportant task to gather together, within the compass of a single volume, choice gems of Thought and of Expression, which may serve to gladden many a weary hour, and suggest ideas of Beauty and of Truth.

The special feature of the Collection now offered to the reader consists in the fact that a large number of the Poems appear for the first time in print, while the rest, so far as I know, have never as yet found a place in any other volume, excepting the Authors' own publications, from which they have, by kind permission, been extracted.

It only remains for me to acknowledge, with

very earnest thanks, the courtesy of those Authors and Publishers who have so willingly aided me in my labour of love. The names of the former will be found appended to their Poems; among the latter I feel bound to make special mention of the well-known firms of Messrs. Longman and Co., Mr. John Murray, Messrs. Bell and Daldy, Messrs. Chapman and Hall, Messrs. Macmillan and Co., Messrs. J. H. and J. Parker, and Messrs. Smith, Elder, and Co.

R. H. B.

INDEX OF SUBJECTS.

		Page
GOOD-NIGHT IN THE PORCH	*Owen Meredith*	1
PER PACEM AD LUCEM	*A. A. Procter*	14
ALL SAINTS	Right Rev. *S. Wilberforce, D.D.*	15
THE TWIN MUTES: TAUGHT AND UNTAUGHT	*C. F. Alexander*	17
HOPE BENEATH THE WATERS	Rev. *C. Turner*	22
"REJOICE EVERMORE"	Most Rev. *R. C. Trench, D.D.*	23
ANGELS	*E. H. W.*	25
OMNISCIENCE	*E. H. W.*	28
TWO SONNETS ON THE OLD TESTAMENT	Very Rev. *W. Alexander*	29
TWO SONNETS ON THE NEW TESTAMENT	Very Rev. *W. Alexander*	31
"THROUGH A GLASS DARKLY"	*J. Ingelow*	33
THE NEW SONG		40
THE SACRED FISHERMAN	Rev. *J. B. S. Monsell, LL.D.*	41
FRAGMENTS OF A LONG-PONDERED POEM	Very Rev. *H. Alford, D.D.*	43
THE RECOLLECTION OF A PICTURE. From "*The House among the Hills*"		49
THE SOUL-DIRGE	Right Rev. *A. C. Coxe, D.D.*	52

Index of Subjects.

		Page
MARAH	C. L. Ford	55
"HE GIVETH SONGS IN THE NIGHT"	J. P. Hopps	57
REST	H. B. Stowe	59
CLOUDS	Rev. W. Croswell, D.D.	61
SUNSET WITH CLOUDS	Rev. G. Lewis, B.A.	63
WAITING FOR SPRING	C. F. Alexander	65
THE HARVEST MOON	Rev. T. J. Potter	67
LOST LOVE	C. L. Ford	70
S. PAUL IN THE DESERT	Rev. A. Brodrick, M.A.	71
THE CHURCH RESTORED	C. F. Alexander	76
THE GIVER AND THE GIFTS	L. Fletcher	77
THE THREE HELMSMEN	A. M. H. Watts	79
STAR SONG	C. L. Ford	83
THE ANGEL MESSENGER	A. Shipton	86
LOVE	From "Tannhäuser; or, the Battle of the Bards"	87
THE HOLY COMMUNION	Rev. R. H. Baynes, M.A.	89
HUNTING THE WATERFALLS	Rev. J. M. Neale, D.D.	91
YOUTH RENEWED	Very Rev. W. Alexander, M.A.	93
THOUGHTS WITHOUT WORDS	E. H. W.	95
ODE TO THE MOON	H. E. Ormerod, M.A.	97
MEMORIES, THE FOOD OF LOVE	Sir E. B. Lytton, Bart., M.P.	99
SEA GLEAMS	Very Rev. W. Alexander, M.A.	101
THE MYSTERY OF CHRIST	C. L. Ford	105

Index of Subjects.

		Page
The Redbreast	Rev. J. H. Abrahall, M.A.	108
From House to Home	C. Rossetti	109
Sunday	Rev. P. Freeman, M.A.	118
Abounding in Hope	Rev. B. Kennedy, D.D.	121
Wonder and Rest	L. Fagan	123
Southwell Minster	A. St. John, M.A.	125
Christ Walking upon the Sea	C. L. Ford	129
Dante in Exile	C. K.	132
Autumn Leaves	J. Andrews, B.A.	135
"Is there no Balm in Gilead?"	C. Sellon	137
Parting	H. Tootell	140
Vocations	Rev. H. A. Rawes, M.A.	141
The Sermon to the Fishermen	J. Ingelow	143
The Battle of the Alma	Rev. J. M. Neale, D.D.	154
Tears	Rev. H. Bonar, D.D.	157
Unexpressed	A. A. Procter	159
Easter	Rev. H. G. Tomkins, M.A.	161
Bread upon the Waters	A. Shipton	163
"In all Time of our Tribulation, Good Lord deliver us"	A. Cambridge	165
The Isis	Rev. H. G. Tomkins, M.A.	168
Wheat and Tares	H. Godwin, F.S.A.	171
The Desired Haven	A. H. Clough, M.A.	173

Index of Subjects.

		Page
THE LIGHT OF THE WORLD.—I.	B. A.	175
THE LIGHT OF THE WORLD.—II.	W. R. Neale	176
AUTUMN MEMORIES	Rev. R. H. Baynes, M.A.	178
"THESE THREE"	Isa Craig	183
VISITATION OF THE SICK	Ven. Archdeacon Wordsworth, D.D.	185
"HAVE MERCY ON ME, O LORD, THOU SON OF DAVID."	Rev. A. Brodrick, M.A.	187
BY THE SHORE	Rev. R. H. Baynes, M.A.	189
JACOB'S LADDER	Very Rev. W. Alexander, M.A.	191
MOMENTS	Lord Houghton	193
VOICE OF THE SEA	Author of "Angel Visits"	195
ON THE THRESHOLD	Mary Howitt	198
"SHE IS NOT DEAD, BUT SLEEPETH"	E. Sandars, B.A.	201
THE DYING SOLDIER'S WIFE	C. F. Alexander	203
GOING OUT AND COMING IN	.	209
DYING AMONG THE PINES	C. F. Alexander	211
"I HAVE THE KEYS OF HELL AND DEATH."	Rev. E. H. Plumptre, M.A.	213
THE SONG OF THE BRIDE	P. J. Baily	215
AT THE ALTAR	Ven. Archdeacon Bickersteth, D.D.	216
THE DEATH OF DAVID	C. F. Alexander	217
THE HOUR OF DEATH	Rev. H. A. Rawes, M.A.	220
EMMAUS	Rev. J. M. Neale, D.D.	222

ENGLISH LYRICS.

GOOD-NIGHT IN THE PORCH.

A LITTLE longer in the light, Love, let me
    be. The air is warm.
I hear the cuckoo's last good-night float
    from the copse below the Farm.
A little longer, Sister sweet—your hand in
    mine—on this old seat.

In yon red gable, which the rose creeps
    round and o'er, your casement shines
Against the yellow west, o'er those forlorn
    and solitary pines.
The long, long day is nearly done. How
    silent all the place is grown!

The stagnant levels, one and all, are burning
    in the distant marsh—
Hark! 'twas the bittern's parting call. The
    frogs are out: with murmurs harsh
The low reeds vibrate. See! the sun
    catches the long pools one by one.

A moment, and those orange flats will turn dead grey or lurid white.
Look up! o'erhead the winnowing bats are come and gone, eluding sight.
The little worms are out. The snails begin to move down shining trails,

With slow pink cones, and soft wet horns. The garden bowers are dim with dew.
With sparkling drops the white-rose thorns are twinkling, where the sun slips through
Those reefs of coral buds hung free below the purple Judas-tree.

From the warm upland comes a gust made fragrant with the brown hay there.
The meek cows, with their white horns thrust above the hedge, stand still and stare.
The steaming horses from the wains droop o'er the tank their plaited manes.

And o'er yon hill-side brown and barren (where you and I as children played,
Starting the rabbit to his warren), I hear the sandy, shrill cascade
Leap down upon the vale, and spill his heart out round the muffled mill.

O can it be for nothing only that God has shown His world to me?
Or but to leave the heart more lonely with loss of beauty . . . can it be?
O closer, closer, Sister dear . . . nay, I have kissed away that tear.

God bless you, Dear, for that kind thought which only
 upon tears could rise!
God bless you for the love that sought to hide them in
 those drooping eyes,
Whose lids I kiss! . . . poor lids, so red! but let my
 kiss fall there instead.

Yes, sad indeed it seems, each night—and sadder, Dear,
 for your sweet sake!—
To watch the last low lingering light, and know not
 where the morn may break.
To-night we sit together here. To-morrow night will
 come . . . ah, where?

O child! howe'er assured be faith, to say farewell is
 fraught with gloom,
When, like one flower, the germs of death and genius
 ripen toward the tomb;
And earth each day, as some fond face at parting, gains a
 graver grace.

There's not a flower, there's not a tree in this old garden
 where we sit,
But what some fragrant memory is closed and folded up
 in it.
To-night the dog-rose smells as wild, as fresh, as when I
 was a child.

'Tis eight years since (do you forget?) we set those lilies
 near the wall:
You were a blue-eyed child: even yet I seem to see the
 ringlets fall—
The golden ringlets, blown behind your shoulders in the
 merry wind.

Ah, me! old times, they cling, they cling! And oft by
 yonder green old gate
The field shows through, in morns of spring, an eager
 boy, I paused elate
With all sweet fancies loosed from school. And oft, you
 know, when eves were cool,

In summer time, and through the trees young gnats began
 to be about,
With some old book upon your knees 'twas here you
 watched the stars come out.
While oft, to please me, you sang through some foolish
 song I made for you.

And there's my epic—I began when life seemed long,
 though longer art—
And all the glorious deeds of man made golden riot in my
 heart—
Eight books . . . it will not number nine! I die before
 my heroine.

Sister! they say that drowning men in one wild moment
 can recall
Their whole life long, and feel again the pain—the bliss
 —that thronged it all :—
Last night those phantoms of the Past again came
 crowding round me fast.

Near morning, when the lamp was low, against the wall
 they seemed to flit ;
And, as the wavering light would glow or fall, they came
 and went with it.
The ghost of boyhood seemed to gaze down the dark verge
 of vanished days.

Once more the garden where she walked on summer eves
    to tend her flowers,
Once more the lawn where first we talked of future years
    in twilight hours
Arose; once more she seemed to pass before me in the
    waving grass

To that old terrace; her bright hair about her warm neck
    all undone,
And waving on the balmy air, with tinges of the dying
    sun.
Just one star kindling in the west: just one bird singing
    near its nest.

So lovely, so beloved! Oh, fair as though that sun had
    never set
Which staid upon her golden hair, in dreams I seem to
    see her yet!
To see her in that old green place—the same hushed,
    smiling, cruel face!

A little older, Love, than you are now; and I was then a
    boy;
And wild and wayward-hearted too: to her my passion
    was a toy,
Soon broken! ah, a foolish thing—a butterfly with
    crumpled wing!

Her hair, too, was like yours—as bright, but with a
    warmer golden tinge:
Her eyes—a somewhat deeper light, and dreamed below a
    longer fringe:
And still that strange grave smile she had stays in my
    heart and keeps it sad!

There's no one knows it, truest friend, but you: for I
    have never breathed
To other ears the frozen end of those Spring garlands
    Hope once wreathed;
And death will come before again I breathe that name
    untouched by pain.

From little things—a star, a flower—that touched us
    with the selfsame thought,
My passion deepened hour by hour, until to that fierce
    heat 'twas wrought,
Which, shrivelling over every nerve, crumbled the out-
    works of reserve.

I told her then, in that wild time, the love I knew she
    long had seen;
The accusing pain that burned like crime, yet left me
    nobler than I had been.
What matter with what words I wooed her? She said
    I had misunderstood her.

And something more—small matter what!—of friendship
    something—sister's love:
She said that I was young—knew not my own heart—as
    the years would prove:
She wished me happy—she conceived an interest in me—
    and believed

I should grow up to something great—and soon forget her
    —soon forget
This fancy—and congratulate my life she had released it,
    yet—
With more such words—a lie! a lie! She broke my
    heart, and flung it by!

A life's libation lifted up, from her proud lip she dashed
    untasted :
There trampled lay love's costly cup, and in the dust the
    wine was wasted.
She knew I could not pour such wine again at any other
    shrine.

Then I remember a numb mood : mad murmurings of the
    words she said :
A slow shame smouldering through my blood ; that
    surged and sung within my head :
And drunken sunlights reeling through the leaves : above,
    the burnished blue

Hot on my eyes—a blazing shield : a noise among the
    waterfalls :
A free crow up the brown cornfield floating at will :
    faint shepherd-calls :
And reapers reaping in the shocks of gold : and girls with
    purple frocks :

All which the more confused my brain : and nothing
    could I realize
But the great fact of my own pain : I saw the fields : I
    heard the cries :
The crow's shade dwindled up the hill : the world went
    on : my heart stood still.

I thought I held in my hot hand my life crushed up :
    I could have tost
The crumpled riddle from me, and laughed loud to think
    what I had lost.
A bitter strength was in my mind : like Samson, when
    she scorned him—blind,

And casting reckless arms about the props of life to hug
    them down—
A madman with his eyes put out.   But all my anger was
    my own.
I spared the worm upon my walk : I left the white rose
    on its stalk.

All's over long since. Was it strange that I was mad
    with grief and shame ?
And I would cross the seas, and change my ancient home,
    my father's name ?
In the wild hope, if that might be, to change my own
    identity !

I know that I was wrong : I know it was not well to be
    so wild.
But the scorn stung so ! . . . Pity now could wound
    not ! . . . I have seen her child :
It had the selfsame eyes she had : their gazing almost
    made me mad.

Dark violet eyes, whose glances, deep with April hints of
    sunny tears,
'Neath long soft lashes laid asleep, seemed all too
    thoughtful for her years ;
As though from mine her gaze had caught the secret of
    some mournful thought.

But when she spoke, her father's air broke o'er her . . .
    that clear confident voice !
Some happy souls there are, that wear their nature
    lightly ; these rejoice
The world by living ; and receive from all men more than
    what they give.

One handful of their buoyant chaff exceeds our hoards of
 careful grain :
Because their love breaks through their laugh, while ours
 is fraught with tender pain :
The world, that knows itself too sad, is proud to keep
 some faces glad :

And so it is! from such an one Misfortune softly steps
 aside
To let him still walk in the sun. These things must be.
 I cannot chide.
Had I been she I might have made the selfsame choice.
 She shunned the shade.

To some men God hath given laughter : but tears to some
 men He hath given :
He bade us sow in tears, hereafter to harvest holier smiles
 in Heaven :
And tears and smiles, they are His gift : both good, to
 smite or to uplift :

He knows His sheep : the wind and showers beat not too
 sharply the shorn lamb :
His wisdom is more wise than ours : He knew my nature
 —what I am :
He tempers smiles with tears : both good, to bear in time
 the Christian mood.

O yet—in scorn of mean relief, let Sorrow bear her
 heavenly fruit!
Better the wildest hour of grief than the low pastime of
 the brute!
Better to weep, for He wept too, than laugh as every fool
 can do!

For sure, 'twere best to bear the cross; nor lightly fling
 the thorns behind;
Lest we grow happy by the loss of what was noblest in
 the mind.
Here—in the ruins of my years—Father, I bless Thee
 through these tears!

It was in the far foreign lands this sickness came upon
 me first.
Below strange suns, 'mid alien hands, this fever of the
 south was nursed,
Until it reached some vital part. I die not of a broken
 heart.

O think not that! If I could live . . . there's much to
 live for—worthy life.
It is not for what fame could give—though that I scorn
 not—but the strife
Were noble for its own sake too. I thought that I had
 much to do—

But God is wisest! Hark, again! . . . 'twas yon black
 bittern, as he rose
Against the wild light o'er the fen. How red your little
 casement glows!
The night falls fast. How lonely, Dear, this bleak old
 house will look next year!

So sad a thought? . . . Ah, yes! I know it is not good to
 brood on this:
And yet—such thoughts will come and go, unbidden.
 'Tis that you should miss,
My darling, one familiar tone of this weak voice when I
 am gone.

And, for what's past—I will not say in what she did that
    all was right,
But all's forgiven ; and I pray for her heart's welfare, day
    and night.
All things are changed ! This cheek would glow even
    near hers but faintly now !

Thou—God ! before whose sleepless eye not even in vain
    the sparrows fall,
Receive, sustain me ! Sanctify my soul. Thou knowest,
    Thou lovest all.
Too weak to walk alone—I see Thy hand : I falter back
    to Thee.

Saved from the curse of time, which throws its baseness
    on us day by day ;
Its wretched joys, and worthless woes ; till all the heart is
    worn away,
I feel Thee near. I hold my breath, by the half-open
    doors of Death.

And sometimes, glimpses from within of glory (wondrous
    sight and sound !)
Float near me :—faces pure from sin ; strange music ;
    saints with splendour crowned :
I seem to feel my native air blow down from some high
    region there,

And fan my spirit pure : I rise above the sense of loss and
    pain :
Faint forms that lured my childhood's eyes, long lost, I
    seem to find again :
I see the end of all : I feel hope, awe, no language can
    reveal.

Forgive me, Lord, if overmuch I loved that form Thou
    madest so fair ;
I know that Thou didst make her such ; and fair but as
    the flowers were—
Thy work : her beauty was but Thine; the human less
    than the Divine.

My life hath been one search for Thee 'mid thorns found
    red with Thy dear blood :
In many a dark Gethsemane I seemed to stand where
    Thou hadst stood ;
And, scorned in this world's Judgment-place, at times,
    through tears, to catch Thy face.

Thou sufferedst here, and didst not fail : Thy bleeding
    feet these paths have trod :
But Thou wert strong, and I am frail : and I am man,
    and Thou wert God.
Be near me : keep me in Thy sight : or lay my soul asleep
    in light.

O to be where the meanest mind is more than Shak-
    speare ! where one look
Shows more than here the wise can find, though toiling
    slow from book to book !
Where life is knowledge : love is sure : and hope's brief
    promise made secure.

O dying voice of human praise ! the crude ambitions of
    my youth !
I long to pour immortal lays ! great pæans of perennial
    Truth !
A larger work ! a loftier aim ! . . . and what are laurel
    leaves and fame ?

And what are words? How little these the silence of the
    soul express!
Mere froth—the foam and flower of seas whose hungering
    waters heave and press
Against the planets and the sides of night—mute,
    yearning, mystic tides!

To ease the heart with song is sweet: sweet to be heard,
    if heard by love.
And you have heard me. When we meet shall we not
    sing the old songs above
To grander music? Sweet, one kiss. O blest it is to die
    like this!—

To lapse from being without pain: your hand in mine, on
    mine your heart:
The unshaken faith to meet again that sheaths the pang
    with which we part:
My head upon your bosom, Sweet; your hand in mine,
    on this old seat!

So; closer wind that tender arm . . . How the hot tears
    fall! Do not weep,
Beloved, but let your smile lay warm about me. "In the
    Lord they sleep."
You know the words the Scripture saith . . . O light,
    O glory! . . . is this death?

Owen Meredith.

PER PACEM AD LUCEM.

DO not ask, O Lord, that life may be
    A pleasant road;
I do not ask that Thou wouldst take from me
    Aught of its load;
I do not ask that flowers should always spring
    Beneath my feet,
I know too well the poison and the sting
    Of things too sweet.
For one thing only, Lord, dear Lord, I plead,
    Lead me aright—
Though strength should falter and though heart should bleed—
    Through Peace to Light.

I do not ask, O Lord, that Thou shouldst shed
    Full radiance here;
Give but a ray of Peace, that I may tread
    Without a fear.
I do not ask my cross to understand,
    My way to see,—
Better in darkness just to feel Thy Hand,
    And follow Thee.
Joy is like restless day, but Peace Divine
    Like quiet night:
Lead me, O Lord, till perfect Day shall shine,
    Through Peace to Light.

                A. A. PROCTER.

ALL SAINTS.

'T was upon the morning of All Saints—
A glorious autumn morn:—The crimson sun
With rays aslant lit up a silver mist
Which had crept on all night—as some great
    host—
Through every lowland valley, but was now
Melting in softest light, like childhood's
    dream.
Above me the clear sky showed almost dark,
So deep its blue beside the gorgeous east.
No cloud had stained it yet, but here and
    there
A snowy vapour, severed from the rest,
Hung high above, as though the visible
    breath
Of passing Angels. I had sat me down
Upon a high hill-side, to see day break,
And think upon All Saints. I know not now
Whether I slept—but so it seemed to me,
My tranced senses sunk o'erpowered before
The glorious presence of an Holy One,
A watcher from on high, who thus to me,
Reading my thoughts, spake graciously:—"Thou
    wouldst
Behold this goodly army of All Saints,
And scan their noble bearing: watch awhile

With eye intent, and I will pass before thee
The sight for which thou cravest."
                              Fixed I sat
With earnest gaze upon the glowing sky,
Where, as I deemed, with all its glory wreathed,
The pageant I should see of passing hosts
Bright with celestial radiance.—Nought I saw;
Only with tottering steps before mine eyes
A meek old man moved by, who feebly helped
The utter weariness of aged feet
With a poor staff. And then on that hill-side
A woman passed, belike a new-made widow,
With her deep weeds—and on her sunken cheek
Sat the pale hue of nights unrestful, spent
In heart-sick watching by some bed of pain :—
Yet on her brow, which the sun's rays now lighted,
Methought there dwelt a glow, brighter than his,
Of peace and holy calm. And so she passed.
Nor saw I more—save that a little child,
Of brightest childlike gentleness, passed by,
Lisping his morning song of infant praise
With a half-inward melody; as though
He were too happy for this creeping earth.—
Yet I sat watching: till upon my ear
Broke that same heavenly voice—" What wouldst thou more,
Or why this empty gaze ? Already thou
In those that passed thee by hast seen ALL SAINTS."

SAMUEL WILBERFORCE, D.D.
Lord Bishop of Oxford.

THE TWIN MUTES:
TAUGHT AND UNTAUGHT.

HERE the thorn grows by a ruined abbey,
    In a valley of our grey north land,
Sits a lonely woman 'mid the gravestones,
    Rocking to and fro with claspèd hand.

Two rough stones, uncarven and unlettered,
    Stand to guard that double-mounded grave,
Darkly brown in the untrodden churchyard,
    Where the starflowers and the harebells wave.

" Ah, my grief is not extreme, O stranger!
    Many a mother mourns a buried child;
Many a hearth that's silent in the Autumn
    Was not voiceless when the Summer smiled.

" But our sorrows are of different texture;
    Through the black there runs a silver thread:
Griefs there are susceptible of comfort,
    Tears not salt above the happy dead.

" Tender joy amid her wildest anguish
    Hath the mother, waiting in the calm
Of the death-hush by her angel's cradle,
    When she thinketh of the crown and palm:

" And the ear that ached with the long tension,
    When the eye gave weary sorrow scope,
Hears at night the voices of the dying
    Breathe again their last low words of hope.

" In mine ear there are no voices ringing ;
    One pale smile is all that memory holds,—
Smile that flickers like a streak at sunset,
    That a night of gloomy cloud enfolds.

" On that mountain, stranger ! where the heather
    Casts a tint of purple and dull red,
And a darker streak along the meadow
    Shows from far the torrent's rocky bed ;—

" Where the broken lines of larch and alder
    To the roof a scanty shelter yield,
And the furze hedge, like a golden girdle,
    Clasps one narrow cultivated field,—

" Lies mine homestead. In that whitewashed dwelling,
    Joys, and pains, and sorrows have I known ;
Looked on the dear faces of my children,
    Seen their smiles, and heard their dying moan.

" Five times had I heard the birth-cry feeble
    In those walls, like music in mine ear,—
Five times, and no son's voice on my bosom
    Cried the cry that mothers love to hear.

" But the sixth time,—more of pain and wailing,
    More of pleasure after long alarms ;
For a boy was in the double blessing,—
    Son and daughter slept within mine arms.

"Ah, what rapture was it all the summer,
   Sitting underneath the alder tree,
 While the breeze came freely up the mountain,
   And my twin babes smiled upon my knee!

"Piped the thrush on many a cloudy evening,
   Poising on the larch-top overhead;
 Cried the brown bird from the heather near us,
   And the torrent warbled in its bed.

"But the twain upon my bosom lying
   Were as dead to voice of bird or man,
 As the stone that under those blue waters
   Heard no rippling music as they ran.

"Silence, silence in the hearts that bounded
   With each passionate pulse of love or hate;
 No articulate language or expression,
   When the soul rushed to its prison-gate.

"Only sometimes through their bars of azure,
   The wild eyes, with glances keen and fond,
 Told some secret of that unsearched nature,
   Of the unfathomed depth that lay beyond.

"Came the lady to our lonely mountain,
   Pleaded gently with her lips of rose;
 Pleaded with her eyes as blue as heaven,
   Spake of endless joys and endless woes.

"Told me art had bridged that gulph of silence,—
   That the delicate finger-language drew
 From the deaf-mute's heart its secret strivings,
   Gave him back the truths that others knew.

"And she prayed me by all Christian duty,
    And she urged me when I wept and strove;—
For the place was far, my son was precious,
    And I loved him with a cruel love.

"Love! ah no, sweet love is true and tender,
    Self-forgetting; flinging at the feet
Of the loved one all her own emotions:
    For my thought such name were all unmeet.

"So I gave the girl, and to my bosom
    Hugged the boy in his long soundless night;—
Gave the life of an immortal spirit
    For the bareness of a short delight.

"Years came, years went, he grew up on this mountain,
    A strange creature, passionate, wild, and strong;
Untaught, savage—wanting, like the savage,
    Natural vent for rapture, or for wrong.

"He was smitten,—when the furze in April,
    To the wind that cometh from the east,
Shakes like gold bells all its hardy blossoms,
    The death arrow struck into his breast.

"And she, too—like that strange wire that vibrates
    Thousand miles along to the same strain,—
His twin sister, through her similar nature,
    In her far home felt the same sharp pain.

"And she came to die beside the hearthstone,
    Where we watched him withering, day by day;
On her wan cheek the same burning hectic,
    In her eye the same ethereal ray.

"But she came back gentle, patient, tutored,
    Climbing noble heights of self-control;
On her brow the conscious calm of knowledge,
    And the Christian's comfort in her soul.

"Ah, mine heart! how throbbed it with reproaches,
    When the weak wan fingers met to pray!
When the eyes looked sweetly up to heaven,
    While my poor boy laughed, and turned away.

"Thus they died. Athwart the red leaves falling
    Rushed the first cold winds of Autumn time,
When the ears that never heard their howling
    Opened to some great eternal chime.

"She went first: the Angel on the threshold
    Saw upon her face the look Divine;
Saw her tracing with her dying finger,
    On my hand, her dear Redeemer's sign.

"And he took her. Softly, without motion,
    Dropped down gently the small finger's tip,
And I looked in her dear eyes and closed them,
    With the smile still lingering on her lip.

"But the boy!—he felt the darkness gather,
    As the Angel's dusky wing drew near:
In his eyes there was a cruel question,
    As he looked up in his doubt and fear.

"On his dying face the shadow darkened:
    He rose up and clung unto my side.
I had lost him, but I could not save him;
    And the shade grew darker as he died."

CECIL FRANCES ALEXANDER.

HOPE BENEATH THE WATERS.

"I CANNOT mount to Heaven beneath this ban.
  Can Christian hope survive so far below
The level of the happiness of man?
  Can Angels' wings in these dark waters grow?"
A spirit voice replied, "From bearing right
  Our sorest burdens, comes fresh strength to bear;
And so we rise again towards the light,
  And quit the sunless depths for upper air:
  Meek patience is as diver's breath to all
Who sink in sorrow's sea, and many a ray
Comes gleaming downward from the source of day,
To guide us reascending from our fall:
The rocks have bruised thee sore; but Angels' wings
Grow best from bruises—hope from anguish springs."

Rev. Charles Turner.

"REJOICE EVERMORE."

BUT how should we be glad?
We that are journeying through a vale of
    tears,
Encompassed with a thousand woes and
    fears,
    How should we not be sad?

    Angels that ever stand
Within the presence-chamber, and there raise
The never-interrupted hymn of praise,
    May welcome this command;

    Or they whose strife is o'er;
Who all their weary length of life have trod,
As pillars now within the temple of God,
    That shall go out no more:

    But we who wander here,
We that are exiled in this gloomy place,
Still doomed to water earth's unthankful face
    With many a bitter tear,—

    Bid us lament and mourn;
Bid us that we go mourning all the day,
And we will find it easy to obey,
    Of our best things forlorn;

But not that we be glad :
If it be true the mourners are the blest,
O leave us, in a world of sin, unrest,
    And trouble, to be sad.

I spake, and thought to weep
For sin and sorrow, suffering and crime,
That fill the world—all mine appointed time
    A settled grief to keep.

When lo! as day from night,
As day from out the womb of night forlorn,
So from that sorrow was that gladness born,
    Even in mine own despite.

Yet was not that by this
Excluded; at the coming of that joy
Fled not that grief, nor did that grief destroy
    The newly-risen bliss :

But side by side they flow,
Two fountains flowing from one smitten heart,
And oft-times scarcely to be known apart,
    That gladness and that woe.

Two fountains from one source,
Or which from two such neighbouring sources run,
That aye for him who shall unseal the one,
    The other flows perforce.

And both are sweet and calm ;
Fair flowers upon the banks of either blow ;
Both fertilize the soil, and where they flow
    Shed round them holy balm.

R. C. TRENCH, D.D.
Lord Archbishop of Dublin.

ANGELS.

"OH, messengers of God, are ye beside us?
　Fair, loving Angels, are ye tarrying nigh,
With gentle hands ever outstretched to guide us?"
　We ask in childhood, looking to the sky,

Drinking its dazzling depths with eyes unfailing,
　Unshadowed by the budding April trees,
While a mysterious, sudden hush prevailing,
　Seems to hold back the voice of bird and breeze

In watchful awe, and willow blooms half broken,
　Leap from our hands, forgetful of their hold,
Because our souls are listening for some token,
　Waiting for some bright presence to unfold

Its glory to our eyes,—in lily vesture,
　With silver wings and dimly-shining hair,
Meeting our earnest gaze with loving gesture,
　And eyes that long unseen have watched us there.

A moment's trance! then, sound through silence piercing—
    Companions shouting from the primrose dells,
The thrush, his half-learnt roundelay rehearsing—
    Calls us to earth, and all the dream dispels.

And on through life, longing for hands to guide us,
    Our hearts repeat again, with yearning sigh,
"Oh, messengers of God, are ye beside us?
    Strong, loving Angels, are ye tarrying nigh!"

And asking so, we learn the lesson slowly;
    Each day's events may be an Angel sent,
With message for the trustful heart and lowly,
    That holds no idol of self-made intent.

Yea, and the daily things our senses greeting,
    The green bud bursting in the dusky hedge,
The solemn clouds through evening silence fleeting
    Above some city housetop's blackened edge;

The wandering butterfly, whose pinions flutter
    Adown some narrow street, in days of Spring,
Have brought sweet thoughts which words may never utter,
    Unto the mourning and the suffering.

The fame of lofty deeds, whereat we wonder,
    And hear in them a voice that calls us on;
The sight of means, whereby good deeds we ponder,
    Turn by occasion into good deeds done;

Angels.

A smile unmasked, a wayside salutation,
   The cloudless brightness of some household face,
By these how often God sends forth salvation
   To souls that faint in their appointed place.

Nor always are they messengers, whose beauty
   Is to our gaze revealed without disguise;
They meet us, too, in form of sternest duty,
   Whose guerdon far in the Hereafter lies.

All hours of sorrow, all distress and danger,
   The coming of a thousand daily cares,
Aye, Death itself may enter as a stranger,
   And prove an Angel honoured unawares.

E. H. W.

OMNISCIENCE.

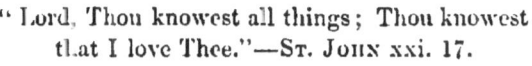

"Lord, Thou knowest all things; Thou knowest that I love Thee."—St. John xxi. 17.

"LOVEST thou Me?" Should any earthly friend
So ask with doubting voice, in sad surprise,
Impassioned answers to our lips would rise,
And fervent words our beating hearts expend,
Yet leave assurance feeble at the end.
Oh, heavenly Friend! with calm though sad replies
Thy servant answered Thee, for Thou art wise;
The heart's deep mysteries Thou dost comprehend
Better than we ourselves; Thine eye discerns
The pearl reposing in the darkest deep
Of a most troubled ocean, and the word,
"Thou knowest all!" to Thee alone returns:
All the past sin, the tears that now we weep,
The speechless love,—"Thou knowest all things, Lord!"

E. H. W.

TWO SONNETS ON THE OLD TESTAMENT.

I.

"Hold not Thy peace at my tears."—
Psalm xxxix. 12.

WHAT is the saddest, lowest, sweetest sound,
  Nearest akin to perfect silence ? Not
  The delicate whisper sometimes in the hot
Autumnal morning heard the corn-fields round ;
Nor yet to lonely man, now almost bound
  By slumber, near his house a murmurous river,
  Buzzing and droning o'er the stones for ever.
Not such faint voice of Autumn oat-encrown'd,
  And not such liquid murmur, O my heart!
  But tears that drop o'er graves, and sins, and fears,
A sound the very weeper scarcely hears,
A music in which silence hath some part.
O Thou, all gentle, who all-hearing art,
  Hold not Thy peace, sweet Saviour, at my tears

II.

> "And the coast descended unto the river Kanah [brook of reeds] southward."—JOSHUA xvii. 9.

The coast descended to the brook of reeds,
   The river Kanah southward. In the stream
   The armour of Manasseh used to gleam,
Marching right up to do those daring deeds
Upon the Canaanite. Wave to wave succeeds,
   O ancient river! age succeeds to age.
   I ask thee nothing of the battle's rage,
Or how the hewing of the forest speeds,
In the land of giants; only I would know,
   Do those old reeds within thy channel quiver,
Making a music when the breezes blow?
   And do their mottled lances slant as ever?
Do they outlive man's strength, God's weakest things,
Of older race than all our lines of kings?

W. ALEXANDER, M.A.
Dean of Emly.

TWO SONNETS ON THE NEW TESTAMENT.

I.

"Then spake Jesus again unto them, saying, I am the Light of the World."—St. John viii. 12.

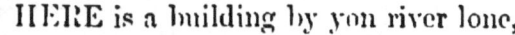

HERE is a building by yon river lone,
    And walking homeward upon winter nights,
    When on the thorn the bitter north-west smites,
    And in mine ear the rustling broom makes moan,
    Or on some mild dusk evening, ere hath shone
    The moonlight on the Mourne, the place doth seem
    A blank and purposeless pile beside the stream.
But suddenly lit up, mine eye hath known
A line of lustrous windows all ablaze;
    A palace of enchantment exquisite,—
    A fairy fabric self-illuminated.
Dark buildings of God's word! with what amaze
    The heart surveys thee, what time thou art lit,
    As from within, by Him who thee created!

II.

"O the depth of the riches both of the wisdom and knowledge of God!"—Romans xi. 33.

I had been reading Paul's great argument,
   Where, after those deep chapters darkly penned,
   He bursts out, "*O the depth!*" toward the end;
When, whether thought or memory might present
Such image—lo! a merchantman was bent,
   Under reefed topsails through a strait to drop,
   Hung o'er with cliffs that almost touched at top.
Dark o'er the wallowing sea the vessel went,
   Till instantaneously she had passed through,
A touch of moonlight on her sails—before her,
World without end, the waves, a blue sky o'er her.
   Behold, I thought, an image passing true,—
After Predestination's narrow road,
The silver ocean of the love of God!

W. ALEXANDER, M.A.
Dean of Emly.

"THROUGH A GLASS DARKLY."

FAIR world! these puzzled souls of ours grow weak
    With beating their bruised wings against the rim
  That bounds their utmost flying, when they seek
    The distant and the dim.

We pant, we strain like birds against their wires;
    Are sick to reach the vast and the beyond;—
  And what avails, if still to our desires
    Those far-off gulfs respond?

Contentment comes not therefore; still there lies
  An outer distance when the first is hailed,
And still for ever yawns before our eyes
  An UTMOST—that is veiled.

Searching those edges of the universe,
  We leave the central fields a fallow part;
To feed the eye more precious things amerce,
  And starve the darkened heart.

Then all goes wrong: the old foundations rock;
    One scorns at him of old who gazed unshod;
One striking with a pickaxe thinks the shock
        Shall move the seat of God.

A little way, a very little way
    (Life is so short) they dig into the rind,
And they are very sorry, so they say,—
        Sorry for what they find.

But truth is sacred—aye, and must be told:
    There is a story long beloved of man;
We must forego it, for it will not hold—
        Nature had no such plan.

And then, "If God hath said it," some should cry,
    "We have the story from the fountain-head:"
Why, then, what better than the old reply,
        The first "Yea, HATH God said?"

The garden, O the garden, must it go,
    Source of our hope and our most dear regret?
The ancient story, must it no more show
        How man may win it yet?

And all upon the Titan child's decree,
    The baby science, born but yesterday,
That in its rash unlearnèd infancy
        With shells and stones at play,

And delving in the outworks of this world,
    And little crevices that it could reach,
Discovered certain bones laid up, and furled
        Under an ancient beach,

And other waifs that lay, to its young mind,
    Some fathoms lower than they ought to lie,
By gain whereof it could not fail to find
    Much proof of ancientry,

Hints at a pedigree withdrawn and vast,
    Terrible deeps, and old obscurities,
Or soulless origin, and twilight passed
    In the primeval seas,

Whereof it tells, as thinking it hath been
    Of truth not meant for man inheritor;
As if this knowledge Heaven had ne'er foreseen,
    And not provided for!

Knowledge ordained to live! although the fate
    Of much that went before it was—to die,
And be called ignorance by such as wait
    Till the next drift comes by.

O marvellous credulity of man!
    If God indeed kept secret, couldst thou know
Or follow up the mighty Artisan
    Unless He willed it so?

And canst thou of the Maker think in sooth
    That of the Made He shall be found at fault,
And dream of wresting from Him hidden truth
    By force or by assault?

But if He keeps not secret—if thine eyes
    He openeth to His wondrous work of late—
Think how in soberness thy wisdom lies,
    And have the grace to wait.

Wait, nor against the half-learned lesson fret,
   Nor chide at old belief as if it erred,
Because thou canst not reconcile as yet
      The Worker and the word.

Either the Worker did in ancient days
   Give us the word, His tale of love and might;
(And if in truth He gave it us, who says
      He did not give it right?)

Or else He gave it not, and then indeed
   We know not if HE IS—by whom our years
Are portioned, who the orphan moons doth lead,
      And the unfathered spheres.

We sit unowned upon our burial sod,
   And know not whence we come or whose we be,
Comfortless mourners for the mount of God,
      The rocks of Calvary:

Bereft of Heaven, and of the long-loved page
   Wrought us by some who thought with death to cope;
Despairing comforters, from age to age
      Sowing the seeds of hope:

Gracious deceivers, who have lifted us
   Out of the slough where passed our unknown youth:
Beneficent liars, who have gifted us
      With sacred love of truth!

Farewell to them: yet pause ere thou unmoor
   And set thine ark adrift on unknown seas;—
How wert thou bettered so, or more secure,
      Thou and thy destinies?

And if thou searchest, and art made to fear
    Facing of unread riddles dark and hard,
And mastering not their majesty austere,
        Their meaning locked and barred;

How would it make the weight and wonder less,
    If, lifted from immortal shoulders down,
The worlds were cast on seas of emptiness,
        In realms without a crown,

And (if there were no God) were left to rue
    Dominion of the air and of the fire?
Then if there be a God, "Let God be true,
        And every man a liar."

But as for me, I do not speak as one
    That is exempt: I am with life at feud:
My heart reproacheth me, as there were none
        Of so small gratitude.

Wherewith shall I console thee, heart of mine,
    And still thy yearning and resolve thy doubt?
That which I know, and that which I divine,
        Alas! have left thee out.

I have aspired to know the might of God,
    As if the story of His love was furled,
Nor sacred foot the grasses e'er had trod
        Of this redeemèd world:—

Have sunk my thoughts as lead into the deep,
    To grope for that abyss whence evil grew,
And spirits of ill, with eyes that cannot weep,
        Hungry and desolate flew;

As if their legions did not one day crowd
    The death-pangs of the Conquering Good to see!
As if a sacred Head had never bowed
    In death for man—for me;

Nor ransomed back the souls beloved, the sons
    Of men, from thraldom with the nether kings,
In that dark country where those evil ones
    Trail their unhallowed wings.

And didst Thou love the race that loved not Thee?
    And didst Thou take to Heaven a human brow?
Dost plead with man's voice by the marvellous sea?
    Art Thou his kinsman now?

O God, O Kinsman loved, but not enough!
    O Man, with eyes majestic after death,
Whose feet have toiled along our pathways rough,
    Whose lips drawn human breath!

By that one likeness which is ours and Thine;
    By that one nature which doth hold us kin;
By that high Heaven where, sinless, Thou dost shine,
    To draw us sinners in;

By Thy last silence in the judgment-hall;
    By long foreknowledge of the deadly tree;
By darkness, by the wormwood and the gall,
    I pray Thee visit me.

Come, lest this heart should, cold and cast away,
    Die ere the Guest adored she entertain—
Lest eyes which never saw Thine earthly day
    Should miss Thy heavenly reign.

"Through a Glass Darkly."

Come, weary-eyed from seeking in the night
    Thy wanderers strayed upon the pathless wold,
Who wounded, dying, cry to Thee for light,
    And cannot find their fold.

And deign, O Watcher with the sleepless brow,
    Pathetic in its yearning—deign reply:
Is there, oh, is there aught that such as Thou
    Wouldst take from such as I?

Are there no briars across Thy pathway thrust?
    Are there no thorns that compass it about?
Nor any stones that Thou wilt deign to trust
    My hands to gather out?

Oh, if Thou wilt, and if such bliss might be,
    It were a cure for doubt, regret, delay,—
Let my lost pathway go—what aileth me?—
    There is a better way.

What though unmarked the happy workman toil,
    And break unthanked of man the stubborn clod?
It is enough, for sacred is the soil,
    Dear are the hills of God.

Far better in its place the lowliest bird
    Should sing aright to Him the lowliest song,
Than that a seraph strayed should take the word
    And sing His glory wrong.

                              JEAN INGELOW.

THE NEW SONG.

BEYOND the hills where suns go down,
And brightly beckon as they go,
I see the land of far renown,
The land which I so soon shall know.

Above the dissonance of time,
And discord of its angry words,
I hear the everlasting chime,
The music of unjarring chords.

I bid it welcome; and my haste
To join it cannot brook delay:
O song of morning, come at last,
And ye who sing it, come away!

O song of light, and dawn, and bliss,
Sound over earth, and fill these skies;
Nor ever, ever, ever cease
Thy soul-entrancing melodies.

Glad song of this disburdened earth,
Which holy voices then shall sing;
Praise for creation's second birth,
And glory to creation's King.

THE SACRED FISHERMAN.

HE gave his fresh young heart to God,
    Nor shrank the cross to bear;
The narrow way of life he trod,
    With watch, and fast, and prayer.

To Him who gave Himself he gave,
    Not man's imperfect good,
But a new heart Christ died to save,
    Washed in His precious blood.

No labour hard, no suffering loss,
    So only he might prove
How cheerfully he bore his cross
    For the dear sake of love.

And at His word, into the deep
    He launched, his toils to set,
Though many a night, while others sleep,
    He draws an empty net.

Yet, at the bidding of his Lord,
    He casts that net again,—
His strength, the warrant of His word;
    His prize, the souls of men.

And day and night he seeks to win,
   As sinks and swells life's tide,
Out of the troubled depths of sin,
   Souls for which Jesus died.

Until the wished-for morn appear,
   And he, toilworn, at last
Feels that that precious gift is near
   Which well o'erpays the past.

The teeming net, which yields at length,
   For labour long and hard,
For broken health and vanished strength,
   More than its full reward,—

In life's deep waters, o'er its shoals,
   Spread henceforth never more,—
The net is broken, but the souls
   Are gathered in to shore.

REV. J. B. S. MONSELL, LL.D.

FRAGMENTS OF A LONG-PONDERED POEM.

I.

WHAT wrath Divine I sing, whose bitter curse
Weighed heavy on the race chosen of God;
What time the Holy City, favoured once
With His high presence, was with armies girt,
And all her gladness into mourning turned.

Say, thou who once above Jerusalem
Didst sheathe thy glittering sword, Angel of Death!
When the forewarnèd king his altar reared,
Humble, on Ornan's floor: for thou dost know
What first, what last, in process dread, went forth
From the Eternal's armoury of wrath:
Sorrow too vast for human heart to hold,
Destruction past example in all time.

But chiefly Thou, to whom the thoughts of men
Lie bare and open, from Thine inner stores
Take of the things Divine, and show them me:
Much sought by nightly prayer and daily toil,
Shine on Thy servant, foolish else, and dark,

And all unfit to meditate high themes;
But haply, in Thy light beholding light,
Some rays of Truth, though dimmed, he may reflect
Into the haunt and concourse of mankind,
And utter forth, in strains of solemn verse,
God's voice of warning to the sons of men.

Tell first, what cause of moment did incite
Abraham's Lord and Isaac's Fear, to thrust
Thus hotly from His presence, whom His arm
So long had shielded—whom He planted in
The mountain of His own inheritance?
For not the murmurs on their desert path,
Massah, nor Meribah, nor those false signs
Remphan and Moloch, nor the offerings vile
Of Baal-peor, grieved Thee, Spirit Divine,
As this; nor all the foul idolatries
Of Israel, or more cherished Judah, drove
The God of Jacob to cast off His own.
Nor yet that day, when Babylon's fierce king
Slew in the sanctuary all the flower of youth,
And burned the house of God, till that the land
Enjoyed her sabbaths, might with this compare;
So foul the slaughter was: without, within,
Inexorable vengeance without stint
Launched its red shafts against the fated race.
Say, then, what cause aroused such wrath in Heaven?

The cry of holy blood: that on the soil
Relentless poured, sent upward unto God
Its dread and silent witness evermore:
Prophet, and priest, and heaven-sent messengers
Cast out and foully slain: but chiefly His,
That Man of sorrows   *   *   *   *

II.

Now had the Son of God His upward path
Accomplished to Heaven's gates, which open stood
Greeting the Victor: He, for thus seemed best,
Alone, as all alone He had achieved
His mighty errand, through the yielding air
Buoyant, those adamantine portals passed,
But not unwelcomed: such a shout burst forth
From all Heaven's armies, now in order bright
Marshalled; and through clear ether jubilant,
Ten thousand times ten thousand sweetest notes
Swelled the full concord, while unnumbered harps
Woke into rapturous music: "Lo, He comes;
The Saviour of the world; the mighty Lord!
All power is given to Him in Heaven and earth;
The Name that is above all other names,
That before Him should every creature bow!"

He through the middle way of highest Heaven
Passed meekly on. Love from His countenance
Shed softest light, blended with purest joy;
And as He went, effulgent streams of flame,
Kindled by recent glory reassumed,
Thickened around Him: Heaven beneath sent up
Her fragrant incense, with thick-springing flowers
Bursting in various hues; with native pearl
And flexile ruby, as a bride bedecked.

Now had the Saviour to the holiest place
Approached, where from the Father's secret Throne
Issues the counsel of the will Divine.
This reached, He stood, first man of all our race
Appearing at the judgment-seat of God;

In death by His own power subduing death,
Spotless from sin; the Godhead into flesh
Not turned, but taking manhood into God.
Forthwith, unwonted radiance, pure and mild
(For gaze, though of the clearest sight in Heaven,
That Throne erewhile endured not), issued forth;
So that all faces, reverently bent
In lowly worship, beamed with silent joy,
The while the voice Divine approval spoke:
"Sit Thou on My right hand, until I make
Thy foes Thy footstool; bring within the veil
Thine human form, thus pure in righteousness;
Be Thou the King and Judge of Heaven and earth;
Stand Thou beside the Throne for man; here plead
Thy merits, and with grateful sacrifice
Be Thou the great High Priest, by whom alone
Shall man draw nigh to God, and meet with grace."

To whom the Saviour thus in prayer replied:
"Father, I will that on the race of men
Thou shouldst bestow another Comforter,
That He may ever with My Church abide;
Even the Spirit of truth, whom I will send,
My promise made of old, now due by Me."

Thus spake the Son of God: and over Heaven
Effluent, as an odour from deep fields of balm,
Passed the Almighty Spirit: not then first
Sent forth   *   *   *   *   *   *

III.

A lone place by the Garden of Gethsemane.

First Christian. A voice from the East!

Prophets (*unseen*). Arm of the Lord, awake!

Second Christian. A voice from the West!

Martyrs (*unseen*). Sword of the Lord, come forth!

First Chris. Seven nights, as I beneath the starry skies
Wandered, in heavenly contemplation rapt,
Have those drear sounds been uttered on mine ear.

Second Chris. Seven nights, in flashes through the
    dusky air,
Mysterious visitants have come and gone;
And all Mount Zion, and Moriah's hill,
Twinkle with sudden gleams of spear and shield.

First Chris. To-day at sunrise were we breaking bread;
And when the hymn, "Thrice Holy," passed away,
Sweet voices in the air took up the strain,—
"Glory to Thee, O Lord most high," they sung,
Majestic angel-voices jubilant:
And then, like mighty forests heard from far,
Responsive breathed unnumbered hosts around.

Second Chris. Hear yet. 'Tis said that some have
    seen the Lord:
How on yon Mount of Olives yesternight
He stood—and sternly o'er the city towers
Lifted His piercèd Hand. Certain it is,
The cup of wrath is full—the doom is near;
The day of vengeance of the Elect is come!

Gabriel (*unseen*). Arise—depart!

IV.

Ephesus. A sick chamber. The holy Angels watching by a bed. They sing softly.

Thou that art highly favoured, once more Hail!
    Not now with maiden blush
    Starting at the sudden guest
Speaking o'er thee salutation strange :
    Not now among thy flowers
    Sitting shaded from the noon, thyself
Fairest lily of all Palestine—
      Yet once more Hail!

Thou that art blessèd among women, Hail!
    Hail to Thy feebleness,
    Evening glory of Thine hoary head,
    Western brightness of Thine heavenward eye,
    Lit now by faith and hope ;
Foremost Thou of all the saintly band,
Standing on the brink of Jordan stream,
      Once more Hail!

Mother of God Incarnate, Hail, all hail!
    Hail, flower of womanhood ;
    Sweetly slumbering at whose favoured breast
Jesus, holy Child, drew human strength :
    At whose deep fond eyes
    Daily gazing, in long draughts He drew
Human love, to blend with power Divine :
      Hail, all hail!

*   *   *   *   *   *

HENRY ALFORD, D.D.
Dean of Canterbury.

THE RECOLLECTION OF A PICTURE.

WE are like children in the meadows playing,
    Where flowers are thickest and the grass is long;
Often by caverned rocks our course delaying,
    Or where the brook is rushing fast and strong;
To far off dells and woodlands often straying,
    Led onwards by the flitting wild bird's song.

A great full river through the land is flowing,
    That will not pause one moment on its way;
Swift to the distant ocean ever going,
    And on its glassy mirror day by day
Pictures of earth and heaven truly showing,—
    The lights of sunrise, and the evening grey.

We, of our fancies hourly growing fonder,
    Like wayward children on a summer morn,
In joy or disappointment wildly wander,
    Fitful as leaves upon the breezes borne;
Nor waiting on the thought of night to ponder,
    Till evening finds us weary and forlorn.

We climb and toil to prove our wanton power;
 We slumber in the clover's fragrant nest;
We fly from flower to fruit, from fruit to flower,
 And linger in the paths we love the best,—
But when our limbs are torn, and tempests lower,
 We backwards turn, and think of seeking rest.

Heart-sick and worn, our feet and hands all bleeding,
 We think of turning back, and finding Thee,
Shepherd! who in the dawn Thy flock wast leading
 By stony paths, through wastes with scarce a tree;
But now, the quiet sheep around Thee feeding,
 Dost pause awhile on yonder flowery lea.

Thou, earlier in the day, our ways discerning,
 Didst call us to accept Thy sheltering care,
Whilst we, with youth and passion inly burning,
 Willed not Thy guidance or Thy love to share;
But homewards now by twilight skies returning,
 We strain our sight and long to see Thee there.

With children's hearts, with children's tears appealing,
 We come to tell how sweets have turned to sours;
Our griefs and disappointed hopes revealing,
 We show Thee cankered fruits and faded flowers;
Or at Thy knees in passionate sorrow kneeling,
 Feel safe, because Thy hand is holding ours.

Ah! pitying One, for us so long abiding!
 All that has worried us we tell to Thee,—
" In that fair grove there was a serpent hiding,

Which, as I stooped, the dew-bright buds to see,
Unseen into my bosom swiftly gliding,
   Twined closely round my heart and poisoned me.

"This flower so wondrous in its pristine glory,
   Which my heart loved as queen flower of the Spring—
I cannot tell the whole long tearful story,—
   How soon it withered like a meaner thing!
And now my hand is wounded all and gory,
   For in my grasp it left a thorny sting."

Ah, blest the children in Thy presence staying,
   Who, when they gather flowers, bring them to Thee!
Nor in the distant fields make long delaying,
   But in Thy range of sight feel glad and free,
And find a joy Thy law of love obeying,
   More happy near Thee than afar to be!
Dear Lord! with pity all my griefs allaying,
   Give this pure life of faith and peace to me.

           FROM "THE HOUSE AMONG THE HILLS."

THE SOUL-DIRGE.

"Then said Jesus, Will ye also go away?"—
 St. John vi. 67.

THE organ played sweet music
  Whileas, on Easter-day,
All heartless from the altar,
  The heedless went away;
And down the broad aisle crowding,
  They seemed a funeral train
That were burying their spirits
  To the music of that strain.

As I listened to the organ,
  And saw them crowd along,
I thought I heard two voices
  Speaking strangely, but not strong;
And one it whispered sadly,
  "Will ye also go away?"
But the other spoke exulting,
  "Ha! the soul-dirge!—hear it play!"

Hear the soul-dirge! hear the soul-dirge!
  And see the feast Divine!
Ha! the jewels of salvation,
  And the trampling feet of swine!

Hear the soul-dirge! hear the soul-dirge!
   Little think they, as they go,
What priceless pearls they tread on,
   Who spurn their Saviour so.

Hear the soul-dirge! hear the soul-dirge!
   It was dread to hear it play,
While the famishing went crowding
   From the Bread of Life away.
They were bidden, they were bidden
   To their Father's festal board;
But they all, with gleeful faces,
   Turned their back upon the Lord.

You had thought the Church a prison,
   Had you seen how they did pour,
With giddy, giddy faces,
   From the consecrated door.
There was Angels' food all ready,
   But the bidden, where were they?
O'er the highways and the hedges,
   Ere the soul-dirge ceased to play.

Oh, the soul-dirge, how it echoed
   The emptied aisles along,
As the open street grew crowded
   With the full outpouring throng;
And then—again the voices,
   "Ha! the soul-dirge!—hear it play!"
And the pensive, pensive whisper,
   "Will ye also go away?"

Few, few were they that lingered
    To sup with Jesus there ;
And yet, for all that spurned Him
    There was plenty, and to spare ;
And now the food of Angels
    Uncovered to my sight,—
All glorious was the altar,
    And the chalice glittered bright.

Then came the hymn Trisagion,
    And rapt me up on high,
With angels and archangels
    To laud and magnify.
I seemed to feast in Heaven ;
    And downward wafted then,
With Angels chanting round me,
    Good-will and peace to men.

I may not tell the rapture
    Of a banquet so Divine ;—
Ho! every one that thirsteth,
    Let him taste the Bread and Wine :
Hear the Bride and Spirit saying,
    "Will ye also go away ?"
Or,—go, poor soul, for ever !
    Oh, the soul-dirge !—hear it play !

ARTHUR CLEVELAND COXE, D.D.,
Lord Bishop of Western New York.

MARAH.

"And when they came to Marah, they could not drink of the waters of Marah, for they were bitter."—Exodus xv. 23.

GOD sends us bitter, that the sweet,
By absence known, may sweeter prove;
As dark for light, as cold for heat
    Brings greater love.

God sends us bitter, as to show
He can both sweet and bitter send;
That both the might and love we know
    Of our great Friend.

He sends us bitter, lest too gay
We wreathe around our heads the rose,
And count our right, what Heaven each day
    As alms bestows.

God sends us bitter, lest we fail
That bitterest Grief aright to prize,
Which did for all the world avail
    In His own eyes.

God sends us bitter, all our sins
Embittering; yet so kindly sends,
The path that bitterness begins
    In sweetness ends.

He sends us bitter, that Heaven's sweet,
Earth's bitter o'er, may sweeter taste;
As Canaan's ground to Israel's feet,
    For that great waste.

Our passions murmur and rebel,
But Faith cries out unto the Lord,
And prayer by patience worketh well
    Its own reward:

For, if our heart the lesson draws
Aright, by bitter chastening taught,
To keep His statutes and His laws
    Even as we ought,

He openeth our eyes to see
(Eyes that our pride of heart had sealed)
The sweetness of Life's heavenly Tree,
    And grief is healed.

And lo! before us in the way
We view the fountains and the palms,
And drink, and pitch our tents, and stay
    Singing sweet psalms.

                    CHARLES LAWRENCE FORD.

"HE GIVETH SONGS IN THE NIGHT."

WE praise Thee oft for hours of bliss,
   For days of quiet rest;
But oh, how seldom do we feel
   That pain and tears are best!

We praise Thee for the shining sun,
   For kind and gladsome ways:
When shall we learn, O Lord, to sing
   Through weary nights and days?

We praise Thee when our path is plain,
   And smooth beneath our feet,
But fain would learn to welcome pain,
   And call the bitter sweet.

When rises first the blush of hope,
   Our hearts begin to sing;
But surely not for this alone
   Should we our gladness bring.

Are there no hours of conflict fierce,
   No weary toils and pains,
No watchings and no bitterness,
   That bring their blessèd gains?—

That bring their blessèd gains full well,
    In truer faith and love,
And patience sweet, and gentleness,
    From our dear Home above?

Teach Thou our weak and wandering hearts
    Aright to read Thy way,—
That Thou with loving hand dost trace
    Our history every day.

Then every thorny crown of care,
    Worn well in patience now,
Shall grow a glorious diadem,
    Upon the faithful brow:

And every word of grief shall change,
    And wave a blessèd flower,
And lift its face beneath our feet,
    To bless us every hour:

And Sorrow's face shall be unveiled,
    And we at last shall see
Her eyes are eyes of tenderness,
    Her speech but echoes Thee.

                    JOHN PAGE HOPPS.

REST.

"I say let the great sea of my soul, that swelleth with the waves, calm itself in Thee—S. Augustine.

LIFE'S mystery, deep restless as the ocean,
   Hath surged and wailed for ages to and fro;
Earth's generations watch its ceaseless motion,
   As in and out its hollow moanings flow:
Shivering and yearning by that unknown sea,
Let my soul calm itself, O Christ! in Thee.

Life's sorrows, with inexorable power,
   Sweep desolation o'er the mortal plain;
And human hopes and loves fly as the chaff,
   Borne by the whirlwind from the ripened grain.
Ah! when before that blast my hopes all flee,
Let my soul calm itself, O Christ! in Thee.

Between the mysteries of death and life
   Thou standest: loving guiding, not explaining,
We ask, and Thou art silent: yet we gaze,
   And our charmed hearts forget their drear complaining.

No crushing fate, no stony destiny,
Thou Lamb that has been slain, we rest in Thee.

The many waves of thought, the mighty tides,
   The groundswell that rolls up from other lands,
From far off worlds, from dim eternal shores
   Whose echo dashes on life's wave-worn strands:
This vague dark tumult of the inner sea
Grows calm, grows bright, O risen Lord, in Thee.

Thy piercèd Hand guides the mysterious wheel,
   Thy thorn-crowned brow now wears the crown of power,
And when the dark enigma presseth sore,
   Thy patient voice saith, "Watch with Me one hour."
As sinks the moaning river in the sea,
In silver peace, so sinks my soul in Thee.

HARRIET BEECHER STOWE.

CLOUDS.

I CANNOT look above, and see
    Yon high-piled, pillowy mass
Of evening clouds, so swimmingly
    In gold and purple pass,
And think not, Lord, how Thou wast seen
    On Israel's desert way,
Before them, in Thy shadowy screen
    Pavilioned all the day;—

Or of those robes of gorgeous hue
    Which the Redeemer wore,
When, ravished from His followers' view,
    Aloft His flight He bore;
When, lifted as on mighty wing,
    He curtained His ascent,
And, wrapt in clouds, went triumphing
    Above the firmament.

Is it a trail of that same pall
    Of many-coloured dyes,
That high above, o'ermantling all,
    Hangs midway down the skies?
Or borders of those sweeping folds
    Which shall be all unfurled
About the Saviour, when He holds
    His judgment on the world?

For in like manner as He went
　(My soul, hast Thou forgot?)
Shall be His terrible descent,
　When man expecteth not.
Strength, Son of man! against that hour,
　Be to our spirits given,
When Thou shalt come again, with power,
　Upon the clouds of heaven.

REV. WILLIAM CROSWELL, D.D.

SUNSET WITH CLOUDS.

THE earth grows dark about me,
    But Heaven shines clear above,
As daylight slowly melts away
    With the crimson light I love;
And clouds, like floating shadows,
    Of every form and hue,
Hover around its dying couch,
    And blush a bright adieu.

Like fiery forms of Angels
    They throng around the sun;
Courtiers that on their monarch wait
    Until his course is run:
From him they take their glory,
    His honour they uphold;
And trail their flowing garments forth
    Of purple, green, and gold.

O bliss to gaze upon them
    From this commanding hill,
And drink the spirit of the hour,
    While all around is still;
While distant skies are opening
    And stretching far away,
A shadowy landscape dipped in gold,
    Where happier spirits stray.

I feel myself immortal,
    As in yon robe of light
The glorious hills and vales of Heaven
    Are dawning on the sight:
I seem to hear the murmur
    Of some celestial stream,
And catch the glimmer of its course
    Beneath the sacred beam.

And such, methinks with rapture,
    Is my eternal Home—
More lovely than this passing glimpse—
    To which my footsteps roam:
There's something yet more glorious
    Succeeds this life of pain;
And, strengthened with a mightier hope,
    I face the world again.

Rev. Gerrard Lewis, B.A.

WAITING FOR SPRING.

WAITING for Spring! The mother, watching lonely
  By her sick child when all the night is dumb,
Hearing no sound save his hoarse breathing only,
  Saith, "He will rally when the Spring days come."

Waiting for Spring! Ah me, all nature tarries,
  As motionless and cold she lies asleep,
Wrapt in her green pine robe that never varies,
  Wearing out Winter by this southern deep.

The tints are too unbroken on the bosom
  Of those great woods; we want some light green shoots;
We want the white and red acacia blossom,
  The blue life hid in all these russet roots.

Waiting for Spring! The hearts of men are watching,
  Each for some better, brighter, fairer thing;
Each ear a distant sound most sweet is catching,
  A herald of the beauty of his Spring.

Waiting for Spring! The nations in their anger,
    Or deadlier torpor wrapt, look onward, still
Feel a far hope through all their strife and languor,
    And better spirits in them throb and thrill.

Waiting for Spring! Christians are waiting ever,
    Body and soul by sin and pain bowed down;
Look for the time when all these clouds shall sever,
    See high above the cross a flowery crown.

Waiting for Spring! Poor hearts! how oft ye weary,
    Looking for better things, and grieving much!
Earth lieth still, though all her bowers be dreary;
    She trusts her God, nor thrills but at His touch.

It must be so,—the man, the soul, the nation,
    The mother by her child—we wait, we wait,
Dreaming out futures; life is expectation,
    A grub, a root that holds our higher state.

Waiting for Spring—the germ for its perfection,
    Earth for all charms by light and colour given,
The body for its robe of resurrection,
    Souls for their Saviour, Christians for our Heaven.

                        CECIL FRANCES ALEXANDER.

THE HARVEST MOON.

SHINES the Harvest Moon full brightly
  O'er the billows of the sea;
Shines the Harvest Moon full softly
  O'er the upland and the lea:
Shines the Harvest Moon full queenly,
  With her chaste and silver light,
With all nature sleeping gently
  In the silence of the night.

Shone the Harvest Moon as brightly
  O'er the billows of the sea;
Shone the Harvest Moon as softly
  O'er the upland and the lea:
Shone the Harvest Moon as queenly
  As she shineth even now,
Though her light, alas! was shining
  On a dying maiden's brow!

Full of sorrow, watching sadly,
  As we stood about the bed,
In the midnight silence thinking
  Of the spirit that had fled!
With the Harvest Moon bright shining
  In her rich and silver sheen,
O'er the leaves of Autumn falling,
  Like the maiden that had been.

Drooping slowly, slowly failing,
    Growing paler every day,
We had watched our fair one flitting
    To her Home of love away.
Through the Spring, and through the Summer,
    We had marked the paling eye :
When the Harvest Moon was shining,
    Came the message from on High !

Once again, so softly speaking,
    Once again we heard her say,—
" Close about me, dear ones, standing,
    Watch my spirit flit away !
Let your voices whisper to me
    Words of hope and trusting love,
As my spirit passeth onward
    To its Home of bliss above !"

Then her faint voice, fainter growing,
    As her spirit ebbed still more,
Like the distant surges breaking
    On the ocean's sounding shore.
With the Angels she was speaking,
    And her face was wondrous bright ;
Then we knew that God was with her,
    That her soul was full of light !

Then we watched the shadow creeping
    O'er her pale and fading face ;
Watched it stealing, surely stealing,
    All her beauty, light, and grace :

The Harvest Moon.

While the Harvest Moon came shining,
   As she shineth even now,
Through the casement—shining sadly
   On the dying maiden's brow!

In the dead-room, watching, watching,
   In the silence of the night;
With the calm face softly sleeping
   In the moonbeams' silver light;
With a sad heart, sadly thinking
   Of the sister that had fled;
With a sad heart, sadly weeping
   In the presence of the dead!

Rev. T. J. Potter.

LOST LOVE.

THEY err who say that love alway
Begetteth like, and finds return;
Else surely all the world to-day
    For Christ would yearn.

Else the dark legions of the lost
Would quick remount their native sky;
For though Almighty Love be crossed,
    It cannot die.

But Love may breathe his hottest fire
On hearts that as the ice remain,
And lavish measureless desire
    But scorn to gain.

And therefore, if with will unbound
The God of love would servèd be,
And love's sweet song must sweeter sound
    If love be free,—

Then may a creature proudly will
That love for ever to deny,
And, by that hatred holding still,
    For ever die.

CHARLES LAWRENCE FORD.

S. PAUL IN THE DESERT.

"I went into Arabia."—GALATIANS i. 17.

AR, far behind, as childhood from a man,
Damascus and her meads, and whispering
    streams,
Her wealth of summer gardens—all are
    fled.
No plashing fountain, in the mountain's
    shade,
Sprinkles each fragrant breeze with pearly
    dew;
But o'er the Desert broods a quivering
    haze,
And the lean sands, in ghastly phantom-
    shape,
Writhe like that host, whom, in their mid-
    night camp,
The angel of the Lord smote.

       Who sleeps there,
'Neath the black curtain of yon stifling tent?
No living thing along those ocean sands,
Save this lost man, with yellow tattered robe,
Half shadowed from the glare,—so like to death,

That but for sighing heavings of his chest,
But for uncertain twitching of parched lips,
Faint throb of sunburnt pulse, one might have deemed
Him friendless robber,—fallen foot to foot
With man's remorseless Foe, while near him moans
His faithful camel, patient in its pain.

Hush! slowly, sadly, from that haggard mouth,
While the dark eyes, beneath a massive brow,
Flash with prophetic light, mysterious falls
The Burden of the Lord, as thunder-rain.

" Alone with God at last!—outside the world,
Its petty round of prying questionings,
Unquiet soul, I have obeyed thy voice;
At last alone with God!—yon far-off speck,
Or ravenous vulture hastening to the corpse,
Or robber plunderer, only makes to me
Arabia's desolation more profound.

" With God alone at last!—In other days,
I knew Him in the records of the Past,
The storied roll of Israel; could feel
How He, The Monarch wise, omnipotent,
Parted the deep, with pillared cloud of fire
Ruled the swift circles of each day and night.
Of old, whole nights alone with God I watched,
Where marshy Issus faced the seething bay,
Could hear the hum of Persian chariot wheels,
While through the blood-flecked pass the warrior fled,
With battle-bow and shield left on the plain
That gave the keys of all the world to Macedon.

"Alone with God!—From boyhood I have scaled
The glacier-fields of Taurus, when the sun
Painted each flushed snow-peak with deathliness;
Or where the Cydnus, clad in virgin foam,
Kissed graceful palms, or citron's scented lips,
While evening sang her olden, touching strain,
Have I not dreamt of far-off worlds and hopes,
By bay or crag, or in some stream-swept glen,
That left no solitude where God was not.

"But this is loneliness!—outside the world
Of earthly love and longing here to lie,
And feel a voiceless wonder in the sky,
As if a Love more high, a Face more pure,
Than hers whom men have pictured in young dreams,
As troubling all their manhood with one look,
Clasped me with such a mighty charm, as passed
The love of women. Oh! not I, but He,
Should speak of Love! that scorching ride at noon,
Dread lurid brilliance, as with thirsty hoofs
We whirled the sands, and I, fallen headlong, heard,
Amid my comrades' shouting, heard a voice,
And felt, as I drooped stunned, a tender hand
Laid on my heart-strings, waking into life
A thousand deep unutterable hopes,
Of one descending from God's awful slopes,
That shine across the blue rim of the seas.

"Oh! love to such as me!—not I, but He,
Should tell of Love!
     Strange Future, that art spread
Before me, where I fear to enter in, and do
As He would bid me:—this unworthy hand,

That gripped a battle-blade against His Church,
To touch the Sacred Food!—to bear afar,
'Mid unknown isles, an untaught Gentile world,
The baptism I have hardly learnt of Love!
How dare I say, 'Lord, here am I; send me'?
And yet Thy love constrains me;—in its might
I am no longer I, but I in Him.

"See yonder old man, with a shepherd's staff,
Wandering through city, desert, on the sea,
Trembling and frail, yet with one story, full
Of Love,—God's love to him, and his for God!
Yet look again.—
    The old man fills a cell,
That hangs above a city's roaring street;—
Outside, a sentry's clanging tramp;—and near,
Rough laughter from a Roman barrack-room.
No man stands by him, where he feebly bends
O'er the planked table, as he slowly writes
To a far Church.—
    Behold, amid the gloom,
On the stone floor a pathway of soft light
Heralds the footstep of a King. No key,
No challenge from the sentinel outside
Proclaims His voiceless coming;—there He stands,
Radiant in love, such as pure woman's soul,
When most unselfish, never dreamt or felt.

"The King!—no longer wearing beggar's robes!
And yet, like one who to high state hath won
His perilous path, would fain look back to home,
To boyish loves, and playmates, fields and streams,
Would keep some poor love-token of the days
When he was all unknown, waiting his fame,

A thoughtful boy, heir of a deathless dawn :—
So, my dear Lord, thou wearest upon Thine Hands
Red nail-prints,—in Thy Side the rent
Torn by the spear-point,—on Thy Holy Brow
The fiery circlet of the thorns !—
                                    What face,
O Lord, like Thine ?—no prison, where Thou art.—
The old man lifts his head,—'tis I myself,
Made pure through suffering. There, before my King,
On the wet stones I kneel ; till The Great Priest
Dazzling absolves me,—prisoner of the Lord."

REV. ALAN BRODRICK, M.A.

THE CHURCH RESTORED.

TOO long, fair shrine! did dull decay prevailing,
    Thy tottering roof and sunken columns claim,
Like Dead Sea fruits, in beauty unavailing,
    The crumbled carvings and the mouldering frame.

Yet from those ashes we behold Thee rearing
    Once more majestic, the fresh fabric wrought;
The graceful shafts, the chiselled wreaths appearing,
    Types of new strength and beauty to our thought.

And may we trust that here is no vain seeming,
    Type of new vows, symbol of brighter days;
Nor idly gaze we, of the future deeming
    That here young hearts shall gush in living praise.

"Thither the tribes go up!"—anew repairing,
    With proffered gifts, our Zion! to thy shrine,
They who have wandered shall, thy blessing sharing,
    Breathe deeper thankfulness in songs Divine.

And pray we for thy peace, O Salem!—Mother!
    Home for the homeless, refuge for the poor;
Blest be the ministering hands that aid each other,
    Thy beauty to renew, thy shelter to restore.

CECIL FRANCES ALEXANDER.

THE GIVER AND THE GIFTS.

THE path I trod so pleasant was and fair,
    I counted it life's best;
Forgetting that Thou, Lord, hadst placed
      me there,
    To journey towards Thy rest.

Forgetting that the path was only good
    Because the homeward way,
I held it fullest beauty where I stood,
    I thought these gleams the day.

I know I might have seen in every star
    That sheds its light on me,
A lamp of Thine, set out to guide from far
    My steps towards home and Thee;—

Have heard in streams with bending grasses clad,
    Which sparkled through the sod,
The music of the river that makes glad
    The city of our God;—

In flowers plucked but to wither in my hand,
    Or passed with lingering feet,
Have read my Father's promise of a land
    Where flowers are still more sweet.

And I have knelt, how often, thanking Thee
    For what Thy love hath given,
Then turned away to bend to these my knee,
    And seek in these my Heaven.

Forgive me that I, looking for the day,
    Forgot whence it would shine;
And turned Thy helps to reasons for delay,
    And loved not Thee but Thine.

Yet most for the cold heart with which I write
    Of sin so faintly felt;—
This frost of doubt, this darkness as of night,
    Thy love can cheer and melt.

On me unworthy shed, O Lord, the glow
    Of Thy dear light and love,
That I may walk with trusting faith below,
    Towards the fair land above;

That I may learn in all Thy gifts to see
    The love that on me smiled,
And find in all I have a thought of Thee,
    Who thus hast blessed Thy child:

And most in what Thy tenderest love hath given—
    Those to my heart most dear;
May I through these look upward to Thy Heaven,
    In these find Thee most near.

                              LUCY FLETCHER.

THE THREE HELMSMEN.

"There are diversities of operations, but it is the same God which worketh all in all."—1 CORINTHIANS xii.

WITHIN my bark I wept, and said,
"Woe, woe unto me! Life hath fled
From my dear helmsman! Hope is dead!"

Night gathered o'er dead Hope and me,
As drifting onward, out to sea,
We neared a trackless mystery.

The keen, forked lightning redly flashed,
Through midnight darkness thunders crashed,
And wild waves madly o'er me dashed.

No beacon's light could I descry,
No star shone forth from that black sky,
As with my Dead I sought to die.

The Past alone to me was clear;
The Present was a realm of fear;
The Future brought no thought of cheer.

Throughout that night of blank despair,
My tears in showers bedewed Hope's hair;
Madly I yearned his death to share.

My hand within his hand did rest,
My lips to his cold lips were pressed,
My breast was laid upon his breast.

Long was that night. At length pale morn
Gazed forth, midst storm-clouds wildly torn
By adverse winds, with eyes forlorn.

Then sank o'er me a trance-like swoon,
Soothing and soft, most heavenly boon!
Nor woke I till the hour of noon.

Then, lo! a bright new silken sail
Floated above me in the gale,
Laden with scents from hill and dale.

And a new helmsman sat and steered
My little bark, which smoothly neared
A glorious strand where palms upreared

Their feathery heads against a blue
And cloudless sky, athwart which flew
Bright-pinioned birds, of rainbow hue.

I lay and looked without amaze,
And looking met that helmsman's gaze;
Then flashed upon me through a haze

Of memories vague, the thought that he
No more my helmsman, Hope, could be,
Although himself I seemed to see.

Weeping, I fell upon my face;
Weeping, because in his old place
I still beheld the ancient grace,

Yet knew it could not be the same ;
Knew that another unknown name
My love, my gratitude would claim.

I sought lost Hope, with mad despair :
His corpse I saw not anywhere ;
To me no other form was fair.

Rather his corpse I would behold,
His corpse within my arms enfold,
Than look on this new helmsman bold.

The glorious strand we soon had passed ;
Again the heavens were overcast ;
Prostrate and riven lay my mast.

Again burst o'er me stormy night ;
Rapt was the helmsman from my sight :
To God I prayed with all my might,—

Prayed eloquent words with lips unsealed,
When, lo ! my bleeding heart was healed,
Through passionate prayer was fresh annealed.

A cadence low, like whispering wind,
Came softly floating through my mind ;
A voice more gentle, tender, kind

Than ever flowed from mortal lips,—
" 'Tis I who guide all human ships,"
Murmured that voice. " When anguish nips

" The buds of life's fair tree, 'tis I
Who gleam forth brightly from on high,
Proclaiming spirit cannot die.

" 'Tis I who sate, ere fell the night,
  Within thy bark as helmsman bright,
  And as dear Hope, thy heart made light.

" 'Tis I who now, as Faith, am steering;
  As spirit now thy heart am cheering,
  Whilst the true Port thy bark is nearing.

" Yet fiercer storms will rise, and I
  No longer at thy helm shall ply,—
  Even, like Hope, must seem to die.

" But let not then thy storm-tossed heart
  Despond; let fear, let pain depart,
  Though Faith no longer ply his part.

" A third brave helmsman will arise,
  Will gaze upon thee with clear eyes,
  Words whispering, wondrous sweet and wise.

" This helmsman, Love, shall make thee blest,
  His strong hand steering towards the West,
  Unto the Port of Perfect Rest.

" Hope, Faith, and Love are brethren brave,
  Who ne'er were tenants of a grave;
  Angels commissioned souls to save.

" Their changing natures ever run
  Towards union in the FATHER, SON,
  And SPIRIT,—mystic THREE IN ONE!"

ANNA MARY HOWITT WATTS.

STAR SONG.

SPEAK to me, lofty stars,
   Low in my prison,
Ere from earth's dungeon-bars
   My soul hath risen;
Uphold me with high hope,
   Whene'er repining,
That life hath larger scope
   E'en than your shining.

Sing to me, happy stars,
   Songs of pure gladness!
Homes where no discord jars,
   Nor mirth is madness!
For here no harp is found
   Of perfect stringing—
Ever some mournful sound
   Breaks on the singing.

Breathe on me, holy stars,
   Pure airs celestial!
Me from my right debars
   This gross terrestrial:

Darkens my flickering flame
    To Heaven aspiring,—
But yours burns on the same,
    Bright and untiring.

Tell me, primeval stars,
    Of olden story,
Earth's thousand plagues and wars,
    And vanished glory:
Ye, from your ramparts high
    Smiling serenely,
Hear Time's dull wheels roll by
    O'er cities queenly;

See flash like falling stars
    The proud marauders,
Carving with scimitars
    The world's wide borders;
See nations rise and fall
    Like ocean's swelling,
And in the lordly hall
    Destruction dwelling.

Whisper me, trusty stars,
    Of things eternal,
The day no darkness mars,
    The year all vernal;
The life complete and round,
    Yet still ascending;
Life that its aim hath found,
    But ne'er its ending.

Star Song.

Roll on, O glorious stars,
   God's praise forth singing,
Light from your golden cars
   On darkness flinging,
Till Earth, emerging pure
   From fire's refining,
Long as your orbs endure
   Rival their shining.

CHARLES LAWRENCE FORD.

THE ANGEL MESSENGER.

"And now men see not the bright light which is in the clouds."—
Job xxxvii. 21.

SORROW! thou art God's Angel! on thy track
   A thousand holy messengers are come,
Calling the wandering child in mercy back;
   Pointing afar, and gently whispering "Home."

Upon thy path we trace the footsteps bright
   Of One, who for our sakes, with thee hath trod:
His tears still gem the thorns, until the light
   Blends into radiance—leading on to God.

Down to the fathomless dark depths He passed,
   And left a lamp to lighten up the tomb;
And now, amid the gloom its beams are cast,
   The lonely valley's darkness to illume.

Thou art God's Angel, Sorrow! though thy face,
   Veiled by thy shadowy wings, is hid awhile,
Sweet is the message on thy scroll we trace—
   A holy rapture hath thy parting smile.

Cowards are we—fain would we pass thee by,
   When thou wouldst wake the soul by sin long stained;
But at thy flight we own thy ministry—
   And find—we have an Angel entertained.

ANNA SHIPTON.

LOVE.

LOVE among the Saints of God,
　　Love within the hearts of men,
Love in every kindly sod
　　That breeds a violet in the glen;
Love in Heaven, and Love on earth,
　　Love in all the amorous air;
Whence comes Love? ah! tell me where
Had such a gracious Presence birth?
Lift thy thoughts to Him, all-knowing,
　　In the hallowed courts above;
From His throne, for ever flowing,
　　Springs the fountain of all Love:
Down to earth the stream descending
　　Meets the hills, and murmurs then,
In a myriad channels wending,
　　Through the happy haunts of men.
Blessèd ye, earth's sons and daughters,
　　Love among you flowing free;
Guard, oh! guard its sacred waters,
　　Tend on them religiously;
Let them through your hearts steal sweetly,
　　With the Spirit wise and bland,
Minister unto them meetly,
　　Touch them not with carnal hand.

Maiden, fashioned so divinely,
　　Whom I worship from afar,
Smile Thou on my soul benignly
　　Sweet, my solitary star:

Gentle harbinger of gladness,
    Still be with me on the way;
Only soother of my sadness,
    Always near, though far away:
Always near, since first upon me
    Fell thy brightness from above,
And my troubled heart within me
    Felt the sudden glow of Love;
At thy sight that gushing river
    Paused, and fell to perfect rest,
And the pool of Love for ever
    Took thy image to its breast.

Let me keep my passion purely,
    Guard its waters free from blame,
Hallow Love, as knowing surely
    It returneth whence it came.
From all channels, good or evil,
    Love, to its pure source enticed,
Finds its own immortal level
    In the charity of Christ.

Ye who hear, behold the river,
    Whence it cometh, whither goes;
Glory be to God, the Giver,
    From whose grace the fountain flows;
Flows and spreads through all creation,
    Counter-charm of every curse,
Love, the waters of Salvation,
    Flowing through the universe!

From "TANNHÄUSER; OR, THE BATTLE OF THE BARDS."

THE HOLY COMMUNION.

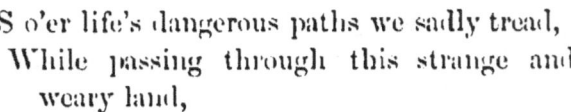
AS o'er life's dangerous paths we sadly tread,
   While passing through this strange and weary land,
Lo! a rich Feast of Love for us is spread,
      By the nail-piercèd Hand.

Fainting and footsore, toil we in the way;
   No manna glistens on the desert sod;
And yet to earnest souls, that kneel and pray,
      There comes the Bread of God.

For us there flows no pure life-giving Rill,
   Such as for Israel's need of old sufficed;
Yet here our thirsting spirits we may fill
      With the glad Wine of Christ.

Resting beneath His shadow, cool and sweet,
   We gain fresh strength for conflict with our foes;
Here the lone desert, with its sultry heat,
      Doth blossom as the rose.

And though these earthly shadows, dark and dim,
Veil from our sight His blessèd Presence now,
Yet Faith exulting lifts her eyes to Him,
 And sees the thorn-crowned Brow!

Waves from the ocean of His mighty love
Break in rejoicing on the expectant shore,
Whispering sweet voices of the Land above,
 Where storms shall be no more.

Glad then, and sacred to all lowly hearts,
The Table spread by the dear Hands of Christ,
Where He His gifts of blessing still imparts
 In Holy Eucharist!

Telling of Calvary and its bitter Cross,
The nails, the thorns, and the spear-wounded Side;
Bidding us count all earthly things but loss
 For love of Him who died.

Pointing us onward to the Day of Light,
When, 'mid the glories of His Home Divine,
Christ and His Church, in robes of purest white,
 Shall drink His own new Wine!

Rev. R. H. Baynes, M.A.

HUNTING THE WATERFALLS.

UP to the source ever!
  Evermore back!
Hearts must lack force never,
  Hand ne'er be slack.
This is his duty, and
  This is his state,
Hunting the waterfalls
  Early and late.

Higher and higher I
  Strive through the glen,
Rough, steep, and briary—
  Well, and what then?
God made it difficult,
  As I may see,
Lest what is beautiful
  Easy should be.

See how they shoot—the rills
  Pure from the mountain;
Man may pollute the rills,
  Never the fountain.
Streams gather fulness
  That pass through the land,
Waterfalls only come
  Pure from God's hand.

On to the sea ever!
  On to the sea!
There and there only
  My stream can be free;
There, where the heaven
  Just kisses the earth,
There will it find a more
  Glorious birth.

Little stream, little stream,
  Dost thou repine
For the pollution that
  Now must be thine?
This at the least be thy
  Comfort in strife,
Gathering fulness, but
  Scattering life.

Little stream, little stream,
  O what a change
When thou art lost in
  The wide ocean range!
Little stream, little stream,
  Glad mayest thou be;
Thou shalt be cleansed in
  The infinite sea!

Rev. J. M. Neale, D.D.

YOUTH RENEWED.

YES; with silver dashing
   Of a shower just shed,
On the gloomy beech-tree,
   Wet were leaves o'erhead.
Wet were all the roses
   On the garden wire,
Wet were all the corn-fields'
   Flakes of yellow fire.

By the gloomy beech-tree,
   By the roses wan,
Looking on the corn-fields,
   Whence the gold was gone,
Walked I sadly, thinking,
   "I am no more young,"
When, among the dripping
   Leaves, a wild bird sung.

Ah! I thought it chanted
   Some immortal strain,
Of a silverer sunshine
   Coming after rain;
Of a richer flushing
   On a finer rose;
Of a tint more golden
   Than the Autumn knows.

Yes, with sorrow wetted,
    In life's Autumn day,
Is the cheek full often
    When the hair grows grey;
All the leaves and blossoms
    Drip with rain of tears,
And the sheaves lie sodden
    On the field of years.

Then a sweet bird singeth
    Of a joy that lies
In the grief that's only
    Glory in disguise;
Sings of youth more happy,
    Sunlight more Divine,—
Gentle bird, sweet spirit,
    What a song is thine!

               W. ALEXANDER, M.A.
                 Dean of Emly.

THOUGHTS WITHOUT WORDS.

WHEREFORE can I never utter
Thoughts that in my bosom rise?
Break, O break the eagle's fetter,
Let it mount toward the skies!

Take thy hand from off the bowstring!
Why the wingèd shaft retain?
Let it cleave the very heavens,
Though it be to fall again.

When the sun looks forth in glory,
Hailing Summer at her birth,
And like footsteps of an Angel,
Fall his rays upon the earth;

When the golden moon is shining,
And the earth is still and pale,
Save the rustling leaves that answer
Mystic whispers of the gale;

And in long procession sweeping,
Snowy clouds move on awhile,
Like choristers in silence passing
Down some vast Cathedral aisle,—

Then my heart swells high within me;
Words!—I seek in vain for them—
What are words? The floating seaweeds
Tell not of the hidden gem.

O the spirits dumbly striving
With the weight of thought unsaid;
O the blind words vainly diving
In that sea unfathomèd.

Where is He the great Deliverer?
Prayerful eye and earthward knee
Supplicate His lips to utter
Ephphatha! and set us free.

* * * * * *

Cease, O troubled soul! thy mourning
That no speech a mirror brings,
Rendering in faithful beauty
All thy deep imaginings.

Weep not when thy sweetest fancies
Pass like silent clouds away,
Unremembered, unreturning,
While no spell doth bid them stay.

They are of a source immortal,
Nor in earthly homes abide;
But with thine own resurrection
Thou shalt find them glorified;

All the yearnings of thy spirit,
That have found no place or name;
All unuttered inspirations
Perfected, and still the same.

Then the burst of radiant voices,
Where no thought is born to die;
Where the fulness of the Spirit
Echoes through Eternity.

E. H. W.

ODE TO THE MOON.

I F thou art skilled, as poets say,
Sweet soft Remembrancer of day,
   To banish unrelenting Care,
   Cheat hopeless breasts of old Despair,
And quite beguile new tears away;

Shed yet abroad a fuller light,
With tenfold tranquil glory bright,
   And soothe my aching heart awhile
   With all the magic of thy smile,
Thou peerless Queen of summer night.

Extinguish with thy glowing fires
The tumult of my wild desires,
   And foster gently into life
   The consciousness of conquered strife,
With calm Content, that never tires.

Shine out to Fancy's happy gaze
On far-off scenes in Childhood's days,
   When Nature seemed without offence
   To Ignorance and Innocence,
And all the world a flowery maze:

Ere Sin had won the charm to lure,
When every wish and thought was pure,
   And Faith, unwavering, fixed above,
   Felt God's unutterable Love,
And all things in that Love secure.

Alas! we slowly, sadly learn
How vainly restless spirits yearn:
   Like thy soft rays of yesternight,
   For ever hidden from the sight,
First faith, first love, can ne'er return.

And therefore sorrow ever lies
In our most pleasant memories,
   For we compare our present fate
   With that which was our first estate,
And weep in sight of Paradise.

HERBERT E. ORMEROD, M.A.

MEMORIES, THE FOOD OF LOVE.

WHEN shall we come to that delightful day
   When each can say to each, "Dost thou remember?"
Let us fill urns with rose-leaves in our May,
   And hive the thrifty sweetness for December.

For who may deem the throne of love secure,
   Till o'er the past the Conqueror spreads his reign?
That only land where human joys endure,
   That dim Elysium where they live again!

Swelled by a thousand streams, the deeps that float
   The bark on which we risk our all should be:
A rill suffices for the idler's boat;
   It needs an ocean for the argosy.

The heart's religion keeps, apart from time,
   The sacred burial-ground of happy hours;
The past is holy with the haunting chime
   Of dreamy Sabbath-bells from distant towers.

Oft dost thou ask me with that bashful eye,
  If I shall love thee evermore as now;
Feasting as fondly on the sure reply,
  As if my lips were virgin of the vow.

Sweet does that question, "Wilt thou love me?" fall
  Upon the heart that has forsworn it will;
But when the words hereafter we recall,
  "Dost thou remember?" shall be sweeter still.

   SIR EDWARD BULWER LYTTON, BART., M.P.

SEA GLEAMS.

[Suggested by reading the section in M. Saisset's "Essai de Philosophie Religieuse," upon the "Existence of God established as a Truth of Intuition."]

1.

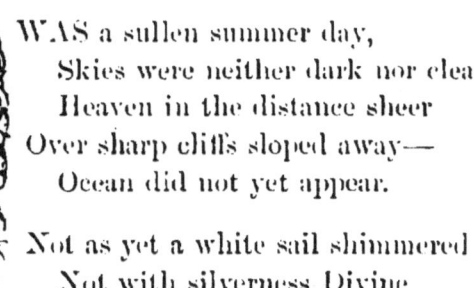

WAS a sullen summer day,
   Skies were neither dark nor clear;
   Heaven in the distance sheer
Over sharp cliffs sloped away—
   Ocean did not yet appear.

Not as yet a white sail shimmered;
   Not with silverness Divine
   Did the great Atlantic shine;
Only very far there glimmered
   Dimly one long tremulous line.

In the hedge were roses, snowed
   Or blushed o'er by summer morn.
   Right and left grew fields of corn,
Stretching greenly from the road.
   From the hay a breath was borne.

Not of the wild roses' twine,
   Not of young corn waving free,
   Not of clover fields, thought we;
Only to that dim bright line
   Looking, cried we, "'Tis the sea!"

In life's sullen Summer day,
   Lo! before us dull hills rise,
   And above, unlovely skies
Slope off with their bluish grey
   O'er the eternal mysteries.

Love's sweet roses, hope's young corn,
   Green fields whispered round and round,
   By the breezes landward bound
(Yet, ah! scalded too, and torn
   By the sea winds), there are found.

And at times, in life's dull day,
   From the flower and the sod,
   And the hill our feet have trod,
To a brightness far away
   Turn we, saying, "It is God!"

II.

AMONG THE SAND-HILLS.

From the ocean half a rood,
   To the sand-hills long and low
   Ever and anon I go,
Hide from me the gleaming flood,
   Only listen to its flow.

To those billowy curls of sand
   Little of delight is lent,—
   As it were a yellow tent
Here and there by some wild hand
   Pitched, and overgrown with bent;

Some few buds, like golden beads,
    Cut in stars on leaves that shine
    Greenly, and a fragrance fine
Of the ocean's delicate weeds,
    Of his foamed and silver wine.

But the place is music-haunted,
    Let there blow what wind soever;—
    Now as by a stately river,
A monotonous requiem's chanted;
    Now you hear great pine-woods shiver.

Frequent, when the tides are low,
    Creep for hours sweet sleepy hums;
    But when in the spring-tide comes,
Then the silver trumpets blow,
    And the waters beat like drums;

And the Atlantic's roll full often,
    Muffled by the sand-hills round,
    Seems a mighty city's sound,
Which the night-time serves to soften,
    By the waker's pillow drowned:

Seems a salvo—state, or battle's—
    Through the purple mountain gaps,
    Heard by peasants; or, perhaps,
Seems a wheel that rolls or rattles;
    Seems an eagle wing that flaps;

Seems a peal of thunder, caught
    By the mountain pines, and tuned
    To a marvellous gentle sound;
Wailings, where despair is not,
    Quieting the heart's deep wound.

Still, what winds there blow soever,
    Wet or shine, by sun or star,
    When white horses plunge afar,
When the palsied froth-lines shiver,
    When the waters quiet are,

On the sand-hills when waves boom,
    Or with ripples scarce at all
    Tumble not so much as crawl,
Ever do we know of whom
    Cometh up the rise and fall.

Need is none to see the ships,
    None to mark the mid-sea jet,
    Softening into violet,
While those old pre-Adamite lips
    To the heaps beyond are set.

Ah! we see not the great foam
    That beyond us strangely rolls,
    Whose white-winged ships are souls,
Sailing from the port called Home,
    When the signal bell, Death, tolls.

And we see no silver shimmer,
    And we catch no hue Divine,
    Of the purpling hyaline;
From the heaving and the glimmer,
    Life's sands bound us with their line.

But by sounds unearthly driven
    Through life's sand-hills, we may be
    Sure that a diviner sea
Floweth to our hearts from Heaven,
    Ebbeth to eternity.

W. ALEXANDER, M.A.,
Dean of Emly.

THE MYSTERY OF CHRIST.

"These false ancilia of man's forging tell of a true that has fallen from Heaven."—HULSEAN LECTURES, 1845.

I MARVEL night and day, and cannot cease ;
  Ask evermore, Can this thing be ?
Heaven brought to earth,—her Maker made my peace,—
  God bound, to set me free !

I cannot love Thee as I would and ought ;
  But, by Thy grace preventing still,
From all things else to Thee returns my thought,
  And brings Thee back my will.

All thoughts, all searches, to this centre tend ;
  All rays in this one focus meet ;
Here, as of old, the wise men journeying spend
  Their treasures at Thy feet.

There is no record, but doth hint of Thee ;
    All history else were false or vain ;
The stones Thy kingdom preach ; loosed with this key,
      All hardest things are plain.

There is no wisdom but doth taste of Thine ;
    All lights that did Thine own forerun
Caught Thy prevenient gleams, as clouds that shine
      In the unrisen sun.

The glories of earth's empires, age by age
    Submitting grandly to decay,
Were but the illusive dawn that did presage
      Thy fixed and perfect day.

Art's beauteous dreams, the charm of thought and song,
    The majesty of rule and law,
The single mind outsoaring from the throng,
      Gifted a world to draw,—

What were they all but preludes poor and faint
    Of Thy supreme imperial Reign
In glory and in beauty, when each saint
      Thy likeness shall attain ?

Thou hast been ever here : of old, as now,
    Walking unseen the paths we go ;
But in the central years, one lifetime, Thou
      Thy visible form didst show.

A cloud did steal Thee from us ; but that hour
    Thy glorious ministry began ;
Thou gavest the word—from thence, with quickening power,
      That word the earth o'erran.

Thou art not gone, but hidden : to our sense
  Thou shalt return ; Thou didst not show
Thy glory at the first, whose height immense
  Stooped to our stature low.

Till Thy true Advent dawn, Thy Church, like Thee,
  Shall suffer, die, and rise again ;
Then, glorified, made white, eternally
  With Thee on earth shall reign.

CHARLES LAWRENCE FORD.

THE REDBREAST.

A BRETON LEGEND.

BEARING His Cross, while Christ passed forth forlorn,
His Godlike forehead by the mock crown torn,
A little bird took from that crown one thorn.

To soothe the dear Redeemer's throbbing head,
That bird did what she could: His blood, 'tis said,
Down-dropping, dyed her tender bosom red.

Since then, no wanton boy disturbs her nest,
Weasel nor wild cat will her young molest,—
All sacred deem that bird of ruddy breast.

REV. JOHN HOSKYNS ABRAHALL, M.A.

FROM HOUSE TO HOME.

THE first was like a dream through Summer heat,
  The second like a tedious numbing swoon,
While the half-frozen pulses lagged to beat
  Beneath a winter moon.

"But," says my friend, "what was this thing and where?"
  It was a pleasure-place within my soul;
An earthly Paradise supremely fair
  That lured me from the goal.

The first part was a tissue of hugged lies;
  The second was its ruin fraught with pain:
Why raise the fair delusion to the skies
  But to be dashed again?

My castle stood of white transparent glass,
  Glittering and frail with many a fretted spire;
But when the Summer sunset came to pass
  It kindled into fire.

My pleasaunce was an undulating green,
    Stately with trees whose shadows slept below,
With glimpses of smooth garden-beds between,
        Like flame, or sky, or snow.

Swift squirrels on the pastures took their ease,
    With leaping lambs safe from the unfearèd knife:
All singing-birds, rejoicing in those trees,
        Fulfilled their careless life.

Wood-pigeons cooed there, stockdoves nestled there:
    My trees were full of songs and flowers and fruit;
Their branches spread a city to the air,
        And mice lodged in their root.

My heath lay farther off, where lizards lived
    In strange metallic mail, just spied and gone:
Like darted lightnings here and there perceived,
        But nowhere dwelt upon.

Frogs and fat toads were there to hop or plod
    And propagate in peace, an uncouth crew,
Where velvet-headed rushes rustling nod,
        And spill the morning dew.

All caterpillars throve beneath my rule,
    With snails and slugs in corners out of sight,—
I never marred the curious sudden stool
        That perfects in a night.

Safe in his excavated gallery
    The burrowing mole groped on from year to year:
No harmless hedgehog curled because of me
        His prickly back for fear.

Oft-times one like an Angel walked with me,
    With spirit-discerning eyes like flames of fire,
But deep as the unfathomed endless sea,
    Fulfilling my desire:

And sometimes like a snowdrift he was fair;
    And sometimes like a sunset, glorious red;
And sometimes he had wings to scale the air
    With aureole round his head.

We sang our songs together by the way,
    Calls and recalls and echoes of delight;
So communed we together all the day,
    And so in dreams by night.

I have no words to tell what way we walked,
    What unforgotten path, now closed and sealed;
I have no words to tell all things we talked,
    All things that he revealed:

This only can I tell: that hour by hour
    I waxed more feastful, lifted up, and glad;
I felt no thorn-prick when I plucked a flower,
    Felt not my friend was sad.

"To-morrow," once I said to him with smiles:
    "To-night," he answered gravely, and was dumb,
But pointed out the stones that numbered miles
    And miles and miles to come.

"Not so," I said: "to-morrow shall be sweet;
    To-night is not so sweet as coming days."
Then first I saw that he had turned his feet,
    Had turned from me his face.

Running and flying miles and miles he went,
    But once looked back to beckon with his hand,
And cry: "Come home, O love, from banishment;
    Come to the distant land."

That night destroyed me like an avalanche;
    One night turned all my summer back to snow:
Next morning not a bird upon my branch,
    Not a lamb woke below,—

No bird, no lamb, no living breathing thing;
    No squirrel scampered on my breezy lawn,
No mouse lodged by his hoard: all joys took wing,
    And fled before that dawn.

Azure and sun were starved from Heaven above,
    No dew had fallen, but biting frost lay hoar:
O love, I knew that I should meet my love,
    Should find my love no more.

"My love no more," I muttered, stunned with pain:
    I shed no tear, I wrung no passionate hand,
Till something whispered: "You shall meet again,
    Meet in a distant land."

Then with a cry like famine I arose,
    I lit my candle, searched from room to room,
Searched up and down; a war of winds that froze
    Swept through the blank of gloom.

I searched day after day, night after night;
    Scant change there came to me of night or day:
"No more," I wailed, "no more:" and trimmed my light,
    And gnashed but did not pray.

Until my heart broke and my spirit broke:
  Upon the frost-bound floor I stumbled, fell,
And moaned: "It is enough: withhold the stroke.
  Farewell, O love, farewell."

Then life swooned from me. And I heard the song
  Of spheres and spirits rejoicing over me.
One cried: "Our sister, she hath suffered long."—
  One answered: "Make her see."—

One cried: "Oh, blessèd she who no more pain,
  Who no more disappointment shall receive."—
One answered: "Not so: she must live again;
  Strengthen thou her to live."

So while I lay entranced a curtain seemed
  To shrivel with crackling from before my face;
Across mine eyes a waxing radiance beamed,
  And showed a certain place.

I saw a vision of a woman, where
  Night and new morning strive for domination:
Incomparably pale, and almost fair,
  And sad beyond expression.

Her eyes were like some fire-enshrining gem,
  Were stately like the stars, and yet were tender;
Her figure charmed me like a windy stem,
  Quivering and drooped and slender.

I stood upon the outer barren ground,
  She stood on inner ground that budded flowers;
While circling in their never-slackening round
  Danced by the mystic hours.

But every flower was lifted on a thorn,
    And every thorn shot upright from its sands
To gall her feet; hoarse laughter pealed in scorn
        With cruel clapping hands.

She bled and wept, yet did not shrink; her strength
    Was strung up until daybreak of delight:
She measured measureless sorrow toward its length,
        And breadth, and depth, and height.

Then marked I how a chain sustained her form,
    A chain of living links not made nor riven:
It stretched sheer up through lightning, wind, and storm,
        And anchored fast in Heaven.

One cried: "How long? yet founded on the Rock
    She shall do battle, suffer, and attain."—
One answered: "Faith quakes in the tempest shock:
        Strengthen her soul again."

I saw a cup sent down and come to her
    Brim full of loathing and of bitterness:
She drank with livid lips that seemed to stir
        The depth, not make it less.

But as she drank I spied a hand distil
    New wine and virgin honey; making it
First bitter-sweet, then sweet indeed, until
        She tasted only sweet.

Her lips and cheeks waxed rosy-fresh and young;
    Drinking she sang: "My soul shall nothing want;"
And drank anew; while soft a song was sung,
        A mystical slow chant.

One cried : "The wounds are faithful of a friend :
  The wilderness shall blossom as a rose."—
One answered : " Rend the veil, declare the end,
  Strengthen her ere she goes."

Then earth and heaven were rolled up like a scroll ;
  Time and space, change and death, had passed away ;
Weight, number, measure, each had reached its whole ;
  The day had come,—that day !

Multitudes—multitudes—stood up in bliss,
  Made equal to the Angels, glorious, fair ;
With harps, palms, wedding-garments, kiss of peace,
  And crowned and haloed hair.

They sang a song, a new song in the height,
  Harping with harps to Him Who is Strong and True :
They drank new wine, their eyes saw with new light,
  Lo, all things were made new.

Tier beyond tier they rose and rose and rose
  So high that it was dreadful, flames with flames :
No man could number them, no tongue disclose
  Their secret sacred names.

As though one pulse stirred all, one rush of blood
  Fed all, one breath swept through them myriad-voiced,
They struck their harps, cast down their crowns, they stood
  And worshipped and rejoiced.

Each face looked one way like a moon new-lit,
  Each face looked one way towards its Sun of Love ;
Drank love and bathed in love and mirrored it,
  And knew no end thereof.

Glory touched glory on each blessèd head,
    Hands locked dear hands never to sunder more:
These were the new-begotten from the dead,
    Whom the great Birthday bore.

Heart answered heart, soul answered soul at rest,
    Double against each other, filled, sufficed;
All loving, loved of all; but loving best
    And best beloved of Christ.

I saw that one who lost her love in pain,
    Who trod on thorns, who drank the loathsome cup:
The lost in night, in day was found again;
    The fallen was lifted up.

They stood together in the blessèd noon,
    They sang together through the length of days;
Each loving face bent Sunwards like a moon
    New-lit with love and praise.

Therefore, O friend, I would not if I might
    Rebuild my house of lies, wherein I joyed
One time to dwell: my soul shall walk in white,
    Cast down but not destroyed.

Therefore in patience I possess my soul;
    Yea, therefore as a flint I set my face,
To pluck down, to build up again the whole—
    But in a distant place.

These thorns are sharp, yet I can tread on them;
    This cup is loathsome, yet He makes it sweet:
My face is steadfast toward Jerusalem,
    My heart remembers it.

From House to Home.

I lift the hanging hands, the feeble knees—
    I, precious more than seven times molten gold—
Until the day when from His storehouses
      God shall bring new and old;

Beauty for ashes, oil of joy for grief,
    Garment of praise for spirit of heaviness:
Although to-day I fade as doth a leaf,
      I languish and grow less.

Although to-day He prunes my twigs with pain,
    Yet doth His blood nourish and warm my root:
To-morrow I shall put forth buds again,
      And clothe myself with fruit.

Although to-day I walk in tedious ways,
    To-day His staff is turned into a rod,
Yet will I wait for Him the appointed days,
      And stay upon my God.

CHRISTINA ROSSETTI.

SUNDAY.

"I was in the Spirit on the Lord's Day."—Rev. i. 10.

AFTER long days of storms and showers,
Of sighing winds and dripping bowers,
How sweet at morn to ope our eyes
On newly swept and garnished skies!

To miss the storm and driving rain,
And see that all is bright again,—
So bright, we cannot choose but say,
Is this the world of yesterday?

Even so, methinks, the Sunday brings
A change o'er all familiar things;
A change, we know not whence it came,—
They are, and they are not, the same.

There is a spell within, around,
O'er eye and ear, o'er sight and sound,
And, loth or willing, they and we
Must own this day a mystery.

Sure all things wear a heavenly dress
That sanctifies their loveliness;
Types of that endless resting-day
When we shall be as changed as they.

To-day our peaceful ordered home
Foreshadoweth mansions yet to come;
We foretaste, in domestic love,
The faultless charities above.

And as at yester-eventide
Our tasks and toys were laid aside,
So here our training for the day
When we shall lay them down for aye.

But not alone for musing deep,
Meek souls their day of days will keep;
Yet other glorious things than these
The Christian in his Sabbath sees.

His eyes by faith his Lord behold,
How on the week's first day of old
From hell He rose, on death He trod,
Was seen of man, and went to God.

And as we fondly pause to look,
When in some daily handled book
Approval's well-known tokens stand,
Traced by some dear and thoughtful hand,

E'en so there shines one day in seven,
Bright with the special mark of Heaven,
That we with love and praise may dwell
On Him who loveth us so well;—

Whether in meditative walk
Alone with God and Heaven we talk,
Catching the simple chime which calls
Our feet to some old Church's walls;

Or, passed within the Church's door,
Where poor are rich, and rich are poor,
We pray the prayers and hear the Word
Which there our fathers prayed and heard;

Or represent in solemn wise
Our all-prevailing Sacrifice,
Feeding, in joint communion high,
The life of Faith, that cannot die.

And surely, in a world like this,
So rife with woe, so scant of bliss,
Where fondest hopes are oftenest crossed,
And fondest hearts are severed most,

'Tis something that we kneel and pray
With loved ones near and far away,—
One God, one Faith, one Hope, one care,
One form of words, one hour of prayer.

'Tis past;—yet pause, till ear and heart,
In one brief silence, ere we part,
Something of that high strain have caught,
The peace of God, which passeth thought.

Then turn we to our earthly homes,
Not doubting but that Jesus comes,
Breathing His peace o'er hall and hut,
At even, when the doors are shut,

Then speeds us on our earthly way,
And hallows every common day:
Without Him, Sunday's self were dim,
But all are bright if spent with Him.

Rev. P. Freeman, M.A.

ABOUNDING IN HOPE.

(Second Sunday in Advent.)

HOPE, Christian soul; in every stage
Of this thine earthly pilgrimage
Let heavenly joy thy thoughts engage:
    Abound in hope.

Hope: though thy lot be want and woe,
Though hate's rude storms against thee
    blow,
Thy Saviour's lot was such below:
    Abound in hope.

Hope: for to all who meekly bear
His cross, He gives His crown to wear:
Abasement here is glory there:
    Abound in hope.

Hope: though thy dear ones round thee die,
Behold with Faith's illumined eye
Their deathless home beyond the sky:
    Abound in hope.

Hope; for upon that happy shore
Sorrow and sighing will be o'er,
And friends shall meet to part no more:
    Abound in hope.

Hope through the watches of the night;
Hope till the morrow bring the light;
Hope till thy faith be lost in sight:
    Abound in hope.

Rev. Benjamin Kennedy, D.D.

WONDER AND REST.

SUGGESTED BY THE MEMORIAL WINDOW, CHARLCOMBE CHURCH.

"CRUCIFIXUS."

"What I do thou knowest not now, but thou shalt know hereafter!"

* * * * * * *

"ASCENDIT."

"When I awake up after Thy likeness, I shall be satisfied with it."

HE saw Him when the road to death He trod,
    She saw His Cross was nigh:
    She knew He there should die,—
He whom she owned the Holy One of God.

She knelt and gazed—mute wonder in her eyes,—
    Gazed on that saddened Face
    Where sin had left no trace,
Till, pitying her grief, the Christ replies:

"I go up to Jerusalem to die,—
    Yet do not weep for Me:
    Couldst thou the future see,
Thou wouldst not shed one tear or heave one sigh.

"What now I do thou canst not understand,—
    Trust Me 'tis best and right:
    Hereafter to thy sight
All shall unveil itself as wisely planned."

   *   *   *   *   *   *

She saw Him once again : how changed that form !
    No hint of anguish there ;
    No 'whelming weight of care ;
No features worn with facing the rough storm !

She knelt and gazed,—calm gladness in her eyes ;
    Gazed on that wondrous Face,
    Where Godhead she could trace,
As slow from earth to Heaven she saw Him rise !

"When I awake up in Thy likeness I
    Shall then be satisfied,"
    She reverent cried :
"Now looking up, I am content to die !"

   *   *   *   *   *   *

The mystery of the Cross is with us now ;
    We wonder as we see
    Christ's life and agony—
See the Life-giver's head in anguish bow.

We, too, must look beyond the mortal strife ;
    Watch Him with trustful eyes,
    Till we, too, see Him rise,
And bid us follow Him,—"the Way—the Life !"

                                       Louisa Fagan.

SOUTHWELL MINSTER.

'T was a gladsome Summer morn, the sun was bright and high,
The birds were singing cheerily, beneath the deep blue sky;
The flowers were all unfolding, and their perfume filled the air—
All nature seemed rejoicing in sights and sounds so fair:

Nor could I wonder, as I gazed on stream, and vale, and wood,
That in the world's young morning God had called them "very good;"
For though a withering blight hath marred the beauty first they wore,
Yet still to each discerning heart there's beauty evermore!

I wandered on with lightsome step, till, from its deep repose,
The Minster, with its grand old towers, before my vision rose;

And whilst I stood with joy beneath its consecrated shade,
I thought of those who long ago in their peaceful rest were laid;—

Of those whose day of trial was o'er—who had fought the battle well—
Who within the Church's blessèd home had ever loved to dwell—
Who found what strength and gladness God surely giveth there,
When at "Matins," and at "Evensong," ascends the voice of Prayer.

Oh! those were England's brightest days, that have departed long,
When all men loved the holy Church, and their faith and hope were strong;
And when, in earnest charity, their time—their all—was given,
To rear those noble Temples — "the very gates of Heaven!"

I stood within its hallowed walls; from many a storied pane
The light in richest colours fell, and as I looked again,
The deeds of love the Healer wrought were plainly on them seen,
Or an apostle, or a saint, or weeping Magdalen!

And as the Choir I entered, the organ-notes were
    pealing,
And white-robed Priests, before the Cross, were all
    devoutly kneeling;
Then upward borne on wings of faith arose the chanted
    cry,
The spirit's deepest utterance, our "solemn Litany!"

Oh! would that those who cast such scorn upon our
    holy things
Could only know the life and peace Christ's true Spouse
    ever brings;
To His one and blessed fold of rest they surely would
    return,
And the priceless birthright of His grace in pride no
    longer spurn.

The Church's Prayers were over, and yet I lingered
    there—
A holy and a deep repose lay round me everywhere;
No longer now I gazed alone on fine-wrought tracery,
For One was by my side whose form was fair exceed-
    ingly.

Her face a quiet beauty wore, and her deep expressive
    eyes
Beamed brightly, purely, like the stars that gem the mid-
    night skies;
And as with her I wandered adown those stately aisles,
I felt that e'en her frown must be more fair than others'
    smiles!

The Minster, with its grand old towers, I ne'er may see again,
Nor hear that voice so musical, whose tones fell on me then ;
But still, the memory of that day, with all its untold joy,
Will be a bright spot in the waste, no time can e'er destroy !

ARTHUR ST. JOHN, M.A.

CHRIST WALKING UPON THE SEA.

THERE are, who proudly throne
    Stern natural laws, progressing still, un-
        aided,
From simplest germ of being, to the zone
    Of worlds in cluster braided;

Who view the hours serene,
    Their ceaseless march in grand succession
        going,
Forecasting what shall be from what hath
        been,
    The past by present showing.

Far back, far up, they hide
Some dim, mysterious Cause, whose word, once spoken,
Launched this vast Whole, that, with self-ordered pride,
    Keeps its firm course unbroken.

Smile on, who vainly dream
Of kind from kind by links unfolded springing—
Faith knows her Lord's bright finger in the beam,
    In storms His footstep ringing.

  And Nature saw one sight
Transgressing sovereign laws, fair Order's daughters,
When He, Who walked in uncreated might,
   Trod the wild midnight waters.

  O wondrous One! I see
Thy Angel-form a light through darkness gliding,
Silvering the foam, as o'er some shadowy lea
   A transient sunbeam gliding.

  Calm as that Sabbath morn
Through golden fields with waves of ripe ears heaving,
Along the watery wave His steps are borne,
   A track of glory leaving.

  As from the moon's full form
Roll back the clouds, lo! His bright Presence spying,
The dark-robed mists, the children of the storm,
   Before Him fast are flying;

  And from the opening blue
The stars look down upon a prouder path
Than ever hero trod, or conqueror knew,
   In triumph or in wrath.

  The sea-birds screaming greet
With joy their Maker; winds wild praise are singing;
Myriads of shining creatures for His feet
   A spangled carpet flinging.

  Like her, as frail, as fair,
Who washed those feet with tears, and wiped with
   tresses,
The fond wave twines its light curls round them there,
   The soft spray, leaping, kisses.

Scarcely to human eye
That sight of wonder and of fear was given;
But all the radiant dwellers in the sky
    Gazed from the doors of Heaven:

And, as they gazed, they sung
Creation's Lord, the great controlling God,
O'erruling, as He listeth, laws that sprung
    To empire at His nod.

                        CHARLES LAWRENCE FORD.

DANTE IN EXILE.

Ah me, my heart is like a dreary wave
    That washes on a wild and lonely shore;
And darkness, like the darkness of the grave,
    Broods o'er me evermore.

An aching void, a dull cold weight of pain,
    A burning thirst for victory never won,
A chilling sense of toil endured in vain,
    Of earnest work undone,—

All these have power upon me, till my heart,
    Thrilled through with anguish, yearns to flee away,
And pants for rest, forbidden to depart,
    Fettered by bonds of clay.

And ever through this tumult of my breast
    Float thoughts of those I love where'er I roam,
As lights and shadows from the reddening East
    Glance o'er the rough sea-foam.

And Florence rises, like a pictured saint
    Crowned with pale moonlight, or the glimmering ghost
Of a dead bride, that with low words and faint
    Speaks of a land loved most.

O Florence, well-beloved in days of old!
   Now longed for, as I long to rest with God,
Though thy fair streets, to me grown strange and cold,
      By alien feet are trod.

O men of iron heart and ruthless hand,
   Ye drained my life-blood when ye thrust me forth,
And ye have made me like a desert land,
      Cold as the frozen North!

Ye hear the Poet's thoughts of thunder sound,
   Know that such dread songs pierce the parent mind,
Fierce shafts of Fate, rejoicing to rebound,
      And strike their sovereign blind.

And though the high Bard scale the eternal gate,
   Far o'er the struggling crowd on strong wings borne,
Swift from the crashing thunder-clouds of hate
      Flash forth the fires of scorn,

Yet I trust on—though tears of blood they weep,
   Borne on life's tempest-heaving tide of woes,
Clasped in Death's loving arms, the great shall sleep
      In most sublime repose.

What though no earthly laurel crown the bust
   Of earnest souls, that toil beneath the sun,
Nor let the sharp steel of their genius rust
      Till Christ's good fight be won?

High thoughts, and noble deeds, that breathe around
   The Poet's heavenward steps, shall guard the dead,
And make their fame a consecrated ground,
      Where no base feet dare tread.

And pure old age the golden fruit shall reap
  Of those whom God hath willed to travel far,
More blest than babes, whom angels kiss to sleep,
    Unsoiled by dust of war.

Our children's children round my grave shall tell
  How Dante fought for faith and truth Divine,—
" Here lies the Bard who sang of Heaven and Hell :
    God rest the Florentine !"

C. K.

AUTUMN LEAVES.

WHEN the harvest work is over,
    And the barns are full of sheaves,
Children in the Autumn twilight
    Gather up the Autumn leaves.

Through the forest rays of glory,
    From the sunset's purple fold,
Flood with splendour field and upland,
    Wave on wave in lines of gold;

Bathing all the woods in sunlight,—
    Lake and stream are burnished o'er,
Glories of the dying Autumn
    Resting upon sea and shore.

Emblem of a life declining,
    Drawing near its earthly goal,—
Light reflected from the future,—
    Sunlight on the passing soul.

Sombre thoughts the Autumn bringeth,
    Of the Summer days gone by,
Of the dusty heat of noonday,
    Memories of the morning sky.

Leaves of gold and russet falling
  In the twilight's solemn hour,
Tell of hopes and joys departing,
  Fading as the fading flower.

Though our barns are filled with plenty,
  Wine, and oil, and golden sheaves,
Every heart hath its own burden,
  Every life its Autumn leaves;—

Hopes that withered in the morning,
  Blighted ere they reached their prime, –
Youth that left us on the journey,—
  Friendships dead before their time.

Then while sunset gold and purple
  O'er the earth its glory weaves,
Let us, with the happy children,
  Gather up our Autumn leaves.

JOHN ANDREWS, B.A.

"IS THERE NO BALM IN GILEAD?"

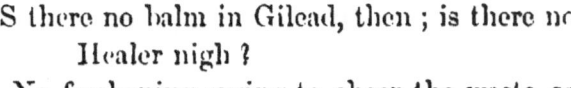S there no balm in Gilead, then; is there no
    Healer nigh?
No freshening spring to cheer the waste so
    desolate and dry?
Hath Hope's dear vision vanished for ever
    from thy sight,
And darkness fallen around thee, the very
    gloom of night?
And seems thy soul forsaken, her every
    blessing flown?
No soothing for her sorrow, and nowhere
    to make her moan?
Yet stay; the cross thou bearest thus hath
    first been born for thee;
Jesus Himself did hang thereon, thy life
    and cure to be.

For thine own ease He bare it all,—the
    scourge and piercing thorn,
    The nailing and the bruising, the denial,
        shame, and scorn;
Darkness and desolation deep, and pangs beyond thy
    thought,
And all for thy soul's healing these sad agonies were
    wrought.

Upon His Cross He yearned for thee, for thee His heart-
    strings brake;
Himself of all forsaken, He could not thee forsake:
Then evermore, when chastenings sore thine inmost
    spirit wring,
Say, My Beloved is crucified, and I to Him will cling.

How shall I sing thy holy love, dear Passion of my Lord?
Or how thy mystic virtue shall I worthily record?
Thou art the spring of all our hope, the balsam of our
    woes,
The solace of our yearnings, and the bower of our repose,
True Paradise of all delights, since joy of grief is born:
For as the flowers but close at night to ope more fresh
    with morn,
So He who wept and bled for us, and bowed in earthly
    gloom,
Now makes those sorrows our bright bliss, those wounds
    our joyous home.

Here is a covert from the storm when winds and waves
    arise,
A shadow in the scorching noon, a light in starless skies,
A staff upon the rugged road, a shield when foes assail,
A charm Divine against whose might no evil can prevail;
For where the Cross of Jesus is, is peace, and there
    alone,
And 'neath that banner of His love He gathereth His
    own;
And thou who wilt be Christ's must not grudge thy
    portion small
In His own bitter chalice, Who once for thee drained it all.

Thou knowest He went not up to joy, but first He
    suffered pain,
And all the selfsame path must tread who that His bliss
    would gain :
Is aught too wearisome or hard for Jesus' sake to bear?
While He is crowned with thorns wilt thou a crown of
    roses wear?
Lo! this good Cross He offers Thee ; it is thy very life :
Anoint with holy unction, it will aid thee in the strife :
'Tis hallowed by thy Saviour's touch, Who hung on it for
    thee,
And Love's sweet might shall make it light, and win the
    victory.

Draw near, thou reft and drooping heart, draw near and
    lift thy gaze
To Him who yearns with outstretched arms thee from
    thy grief to raise ;
Draw near, and clinging close beneath thy Saviour's
    bleeding heart,
Tell o'er each throb of that deep woe in which thou hast
    a part ;
Tell o'er each drop of dear life-blood which ebbs for thee
    so fast,
And all thy weary heart-aching upon that true Love cast :
In Jesu's Cross and Passion is the medicine of thy soul,
Yea, there is balm in Gilead, and a Healer to make
    whole.

                                      C. SELLON.

PARTING.

As we see the sun in Spring-time
   Shine with warm life-giving ray,
For a moment lighting all things,
   Then so sadly fade away;

So on earth, true friendship's blessing
   Sheds on us its warmth and light;
Yet, ere we can catch its treasure,
   Flying, leaves us dark as night.

Streams divided flow no longer
   In communion side by side;
Who can say where they shall mingle,—
   Here, or in the ocean tide?

Here, the scene of restless wandering,
   Where with pain and toil we rove:
There, the everlasting gladness,
   The ocean tide of Heavenly Love.

                HENRY TOOTELL,
                    University College, Oxon.

VOCATIONS.

HERE marches past a mighty ordered band,
   Upon whose banners the full light is shed;
   It leaves the charnel-houses of the dead,
And goes straight onward to the far-off Land.

Kept from all baser wants and mean desires,
   They lead the way, on whom the Light has shone
   With purest strength; by this bright way have gone
All who have clearly seen the beacon-fires.

Those fires upon the battlements of gold
   Burn with unclouded glory, and their gleam
   Falls on the warriors like a fiery stream,
A light and warmth in darkness and in cold.

Yet noble souls lie often in the dust,
   By their own fault, when they might rise to God:
   On them in fire is written Ichabod,
For light despised and weapons brown with rust.

No generous love has led them on to Him,
   Who went for them along the mournful way,
   And bore the heat and burden of the day:
For this their hearts are cold, their eyes are dim.

Yet light of Heaven all light of earth outshines:
   Strange then that in the slothful ways of ease
   Men should be lost, as if in stormy seas,
When all the earth is lit with altar-shrines.

He that hath ears must hear, for now there rings
   Deep in men's hearts, as all can hear who will,
   A strong, clear Voice, that one day it may fill
With Saints the City of the King of kings.

Some hear that Voice and heed it not, but stand
   Immoveable in darkness, making choice
   Of the way downward, though they hear the Voice,
False-hearted traitors to their King's command.

Some hear, and gladly follow for a while,
   With sandalled feet upon the royal road,
   Seeing its light; then blinded turn from God,
And with dark cowardice their souls defile.

But some who hear are faithful and obey;
   Called and elect and true, with spears of light
   And shining armour, through the storm and night,
They bear their lilied standards to the Day.

Pray to be blinded to the world's strong glare;
   Pray to see brightly the clear Heaven above;
   For they are highest on its thrones of love
Who most for God in this dark world will dare.

Before us goes the strong Incarnate Word;
   In Him the weak ones overcome the strong;
   Thus in His strength the Cross is borne along,
Thus onward sweep the armies of the Lord.

                    Rev. H. A. Rawes, M.A.

THE SERMON TO THE FISHERMEN.

"Behold, I stand at the door, and knock."—
REVELATION iii. 20.

SEE! I will show at whose unopened doors
He stands and knocks, that you may never
say,
"I am too mean, too ignorant, too lost;
He knocks at other doors, but not at
mine!"

'See here! it is the night! it is the night!
And snow lies thickly, white untrodden snow,
And the wan moon upon a casement shines—
A casement crusted o'er with frosty leaves,
That make her ray less bright along the floor.
A woman sits, with hands upon her knees,
Poor tired soul! and she has nought to do,
For there is neither fire nor candle light:
The driftwood ash lies cold upon her hearth;
The rushlight flickered down an hour ago;
Her children wail a little in their sleep
For cold and hunger, and, as if that sound
Was not enough, another comes to her,
Over God's undefiled snow—a song—
Nay, never hang your heads—I say, a song.

And doth she curse the alehouse, and the sots
That drink the night out and their earnings there,
And drink their manly strength and courage down,
And drink away the little children's bread,
And starve her, starving by the selfsame act
Her tender suckling, that with piteous eyes
Looks in her face till scarcely she has heart
To work, and earn the scanty bit and drop
That feed the others?
     Does she curse the song?
I think not, fishermen; I have not heard
Such women curse. God's curse is curse enough.
To-morrow she will say a bitter thing,
Pulling her sleeve down lest the bruises show—
A bitter thing, but meant for an excuse—
"My master is not worse than many men:"
But now, ay, now she sitteth dumb and still;
No food, no comfort, cold and poverty
Bearing her down.
    My heart is sore for her;
How long, how long? When troubles come of God,
When men are frozen out of work, when wives
Are sick, when working fathers fail and die,
When boats go down at sea—then nought behoves
Like patience; but for troubles wrought of men
Patience is hard—I tell you it is hard.

' O thou poor soul! it is the night—the night;
Against thy door drifts up the silent snow,
Blocking thy threshold: "Fall," thou sayest, "fall, fall,
Cold snow, and lie and be trod underfoot,—
Am not I fallen? Wake up, and pipe, O wind,

Dull wind, and beat and bluster at my door:
Merciful wind, sing me a hoarse rough song,
For there is other music made to-night
That I would fain not hear. Wake, thou still sea,
Heavily plunge. Shoot on, white waterfall.
Oh, I could long like thy cold icicles
Freeze, freeze, and hang upon thy frosty clift,
And not complain, so I might melt at last
In the warm Summer sun, as thou wilt do!

'"But woe is me! I think there is no sun;
My sun is sunken, and the night grows dark:
None care for me. The children cry for bread,
And I have none, and nought can comfort me;
Even if the heavens were free to such as I,
It were not much, for death is long to wait,
And Heaven is far to go!"

      And speakest thou thus,
Despairing of the sun that sets to thee,
And of the earthly love that wanes to thee,
And of the Heaven that lieth far from thee?
Peace, peace, fond fool! One draweth near thy door
Whose footsteps leave no print across the snow:
Thy sun has risen with comfort in his face,
The smile of Heaven, to warm thy frozen heart
And bless with saintly hand. What! is it long
To wait and far to go? Thou shalt not go;
Behold, across the snow to thee He comes;'
Thy Heaven descends, and is it long to wait?
Thou shalt not wait: "This night, this night," He saith,
"I stand at the door and knock."

L.

'It is enough—can such an one be here—
Yea, here? O God forgive you, fishermen!
One! is there only one? But do thou know,
O woman pale for want, if thou art here,
That on thy lot much thought is spent in Heaven:
And, coveting the heart a hard man broke,
One standeth patient, watching in the night,
And waiting in the daytime.
      What shall be
If thou wilt answer? He will smile on thee:
One smile of His shall be enough to heal
The wound of man's neglect; and He will sigh,
Pitying the trouble which that sigh shall cure;
And He will speak—speak in the desolate night,
In the dark night: "For Me a thorny crown
Men wove, and nails were driven in My hands
And feet: there was an earthquake, and I died;
I died, and am alive for evermore!

'"I died for thee; for thee I am alive,
And My humanity doth mourn for thee,
For thou art Mine; and all thy little ones,
They, too, are Mine, are Mine! Behold, the house
Is dark, but there is brightness where the sons
Of God are singing, and, behold, the heart
Is troubled: yet the nations walk in white;
They have forgotten how to weep; and thou
Shalt also come, and I will foster thee
And satisfy thy soul; and thou shalt warm
Thy trembling life beneath the smile of God.
A little while—it is a little while—
A little while, and I will comfort thee;
I go away, but I will come again."

' But hear me yet. There was a poor old man
Who sat and listened to the raging sea,
And heard it thunder, lunging at the cliffs
As like to tear them down. He lay at night;
And " Lord have mercy on the lads," said he,
" That sailed at noon, though they be none of mine!
For when the gale gets up, and when the wind
Flings at the window, when it beats the roof,
And lulls, and stops, and rouses up again,
And cuts the crest clean off the plunging wave,
And scatters it like feathers up the field,
Why, then I think of my two lads—my lads
That would have worked and never let me want,
And never let me take the parish pay.
No, none of mine; my lads were drowned at sea—
My two—before the most of these were born.
I know how sharp that cuts, since my poor wife
Walked up and down, and still walked up and down,
And I walked after, and one could not hear
A word the other said, for wind and sea
That raged and beat and thundered in the night—
The awfullest, the longest, lightest night
That ever parents had to spend—a moon
That shone like daylight on the breaking wave.
Ah me! and other men have lost their lads,
And other women wiped their poor dead mouths,
And got them home and dried them in the house,
And seen the driftwood lie along the coast,
That was a tidy boat but one day back,
And seen next tide the neighbours gather it
To lay it on their fires.

                              Ay, I was strong
And able-bodied—loved my work ;—but now
I am a useless hull : 'tis time I sunk ;
I am in all men's way ; I trouble them ;
I am a trouble to myself : but yet
I feel for mariners of stormy nights,
And feel for wives that watch ashore. Ay, ay !
If I had learning I would pray the Lord
To bring them in: but I'm no scholar, no ;
Book-learning is a world too hard for me :
But I make bold to say, ' O Lord, good Lord,
I am a broken-down poor man, a fool
To speak to Thee : but in the Book 'tis writ,
As I hear say from others that can read,
How, when Thou camest, Thou didst love the sea,
And live with fisherfolk, whereby 'tis sure
Thou knowest all the peril they go through,
And all their trouble.
                        As for me, good Lord,
I have no boat ; I am too old, too old—
My lads are drowned ; I buried my poor wife ;
My little lasses died so long ago
That mostly I forget what they were like.
Thou knowest, Lord ; they were such little ones
I know they went to Thee, but I forget
Their faces, though I missed them sore.
                                         O Lord,
I was a strong man ; I have drawn good food
And made good money out of Thy great sea:
But yet I cried for them at nights ; and now,
Although I be so old, I miss my lads,
And there be many folk this stormy night

Heavy with fear for theirs. Merciful Lord,
Comfort them; save their honest boys, their pride,
And let them hear next ebb the blessedest,
Best sound—the boat-keels grating on the sand.'

' " I cannot pray with finer words : I know
Nothing; I have no learning, cannot learn—
Too old, too old. They say I want for nought,
I have the parish pay ; but I am dull
Of hearing, and the fire scarce warms me through.
God save me—I have been a sinful man—
And save the lives of them that still can work,
For they are good to me ; ay, good to me.
But, Lord, I am a trouble! and I sit,
And I am lonesome, and the nights are few
That any think to come and draw a chair,
And sit in my poor place and talk awhile.
Why should they come, forsooth ? Only the wind
Knocks at my door, oh, long and loud it knocks,
The only thing God made that has a mind
To enter in."

  ' Yea, thus the old man spake :
These were the last words of his aged mouth—
BUT ONE DID KNOCK. One came to sup with him,
That humble, weak old man ; knocked at his door
In the rough pauses of the labouring wind.
I tell you that One knocked while it was dark,
Save where their foaming passion had made white
Those livid seething billows. What He said
In that poor place where He did talk awhile,
I cannot tell : but this I am assured,
That when the neighbours came the morrow morn,

What time the wind had bated, and the sun
Shone on the old man's floor, they saw the smile
He passed away in, and they said, " He looks
As he had woke and seen the face of Christ,
And with that rapturous smile held out his arms
To come to Him!"

                  Can such an one be here,
So old, so weak, so ignorant, so frail?
The Lord be good to thee, thou poor old man;
It would be hard with thee if Heaven were shut
To such as have not learning! Nay, nay, nay,
He condescends to them of low estate;
To such as are despised He cometh down,
Stands at the door and knocks.

                    Yet bear with me.
I have a message; I have more to say.
Shall sorrow win His pity, and not sin—
That burden ten times heavier to be borne?
What think you? Shall the virtuous have His care
Alone? O virtuous women, think not scorn,
For you may lift your faces everywhere;
And now that it grows dusk, and I can see
None though they front me straight, I fain would tell
A certain thing to you. I say to you;
And if it doth concern you, as methinks
It doth, then surely it concerneth all.
I say that there was once—I say not here—
I say that there was once a castaway,
And she was weeping, weeping bitterly;
Kneeling, and crying with a heart-sick cry

That choked itself in sobs—" O my good name !
O my good name !". And none did hear her cry !
Nay ; and it lightened, and the storm-bolts fell,
And the rain splashed upon the roof, and still
She, storm-tossed as the storming elements—
She cried with an exceeding bitter cry,
" O my good name !" And then the thunder-cloud
Stooped low and burst in darkness overhead,
And rolled, and rocked her on her knees, and shook
The frail foundations of her dwelling-place.
But she—if any neighbour had come in
(None did): if any neighbours had come in,
They might have seen her crying on her knees,
And sobbing " Lost, lost, lost !" beating her breast—
Her breast for ever pricked with cruel thorns,
The wounds whereof could neither balm assuage
Nor any patience heal—beating her brow,
Which ached, it had been bent so long to hide
From level eyes, whose meaning was contempt.

' O ye good women, it is hard to leave
The paths of virtue, and return again.
What if this sinner wept, and none of you
Comforted her ? And what if she did strive
To mend, and none of you believed her strife,
Nor looked upon her ? Mark, I do not say,
Though it was hard, you therefore were to blame—
That she had aught against you, though your feet
Never drew near her door. But I beseech
Your patience. Once in Old Jerusalem
A woman kneeled at consecrated feet,
Kissed them, and washed them with her tears.

       What then?
I think that yet our Lord is pitiful:
I think I see the castaway e'en now!
And she is not alone: the heavy rain
Splashes without, and sullen thunder rolls,
But she is lying at the sacred feet
Of One transfigured.
      And her tears flow down,
Down to her lips—her lips that kiss the print
Of nails; and love is like to break her heart!
Love and repentance—for it still doth work
Sore in her soul to think, to think that she,
Even she, did pierce the sacred, sacred feet,
And bruise the thorn-crowned head.
       O Lord, our Lord,
How great is thy compassion! Come, good Lord,
For we will open. Come this night, good Lord;
Stand at the door and knock.
       And is this all?—
Trouble, old age, and simpleness, and sin—
This all? It might be all some other night;
But this night, if a voice said, "Give account,
Whom hast thou with thee?" then must I reply,
"Young manhood have I, beautiful youth and strength,
Rich with all treasure drawn up from the crypt
Where lies the learning of the ancient world;
Brave with all thoughts that poets fling upon
The strand of life, as driftweed after storms:
Doubtless familiar with Thy mountain heads,
And the dread purity of Alpine snows,
Doubtless familiar with Thy works concealed
For ages from mankind—outlying worlds,

And many moonèd spheres—and Thy great store
Of stars, more thick than mealy dust which here
Powders the pale leaves of Auriculas.

This do I know, but, Lord, I know not more.

Not more concerning them—concerning Thee
I know Thy bounty : where Thou givest much
Standing without, if any call Thee in
Thou givest more." Speak, then, O rich and strong :
Open, O happy young, ere yet the hand
Of Him that knocks, wearied at last, forbear ;
The patient foot its thankless quest refrain,
The wounded heart for evermore withdraw.'

I have heard many speak, but this one man—
So anxious not to go to Heaven alone—
This one man I remember, and his look,
Till twilight overshadowed him. He ceased,
And out in darkness with the fisher folk
We passed, and stumbled over mounds of moss,
And heard, but did not see, the passing beck.
Ah, graceless heart, would that it could regain,
From the dim storehouse of sensations past,
The impress full of tender awe, that night,
Which fell on me! It was as if the Christ
Had been drawn down from Heaven to track us home,
And any of the footsteps following us
Might have been His.

JEAN INGELOW.

THE BATTLE OF THE ALMA.

BY the faint and dying watchfires,
　　Wounded, harassed, wearied out,
If ye hear the vengeful trumpet,
　　If ye catch the foeman's shout,—

What great wonder, though the Eagle
　　Russia crushed in height of pride,
Should to-day have better fortune
　　With the Leopard at its side ?

Think, beside the Borodino,
　　How, where ninety thousand lay,
Russian peasants kept the Old Guard
　　Twelve long dreadful hours at bay :

When we fired our holy Moscow,
　　How, behind their rout and rack,
Hung the lances of the Ukraine,
　　And the vengeful Don Cossack !

If this world were all, how glorious
　　Was that storming of the height,
With the Chasseurs in the centre,
　　And the Life Guard to the right !

When around the dying Marshal
    Formed the line and rose the cheers,—
Him that trapped and burned the captives
    In the cave beside Algiers.

Though outnumbered, out-manœuvred,
    Something comforts us within,
Whispering,—It is sometimes nobler
    To be conquered than to win ;—

Nobler to be conquered, falling
    For each home, and wife, and pet,—
Nobler to be conquered, leaving
    Names our land will not forget ;—

Nobler as our priests to perish,
    Dying when they could no more ;
And our Sisters of S. Basil,
    Nursing ancle deep in gore :

Than for greed of gold and glory
    On the hard won field to say,
God Himself approves aggression,
    For to Him we owe the day.

France and England ! sing Te Deum
    O'er the hopes by you defaced ;
O'er the homes by you made childless ;
    O'er the hearths by you laid waste :

And, to serve both God and Mammon—
    This world's gain, but that world's loss -
High above your very altars
    Wreathe the Crescent with the Cross.

There is One by whom this action
  Shall hereafter be repaid,—
Truer scales than those of glory,
  Where this battle shall be weighed.

On the Vigil of S. Matthew,
  Russian hearts shall ever pray
For the men that died by Alma,
  When the Crescent won the day.

Courage, brethren,—France's tyrant,
  Through the good path ope'd by you,
May have yet his S. Helena,
  Alma yet her Waterloo!

Rev. J. M. Neale, D.D.

TEARS.

TEARS are not always fruitful; their hot drops
   Sometimes but scorch the cheek and dim the eye;
Despairing murmurs over blackened hopes,
   Not the meek spirit's calm and chastened cry.

Oh, better not to weep than weep amiss;
   For hard it is to learn to weep aright,—
To weep wise tears, the tears that heal and bless,
   The tears which their own bitterness requite.

Oh, better not to grieve than waste our woe;
   To fling away the spirit's finest gold;
To lose, not gain, by sorrow; to overflow
   The sacred channels which true sadness hold.

To shed our tears as trees their blossoms shed,
   Not all at random, but to make sure way
For fruit in season, when the bloom lies dead
   On the chill earth, the victim of decay;—

This is to use the grief that God has sent,
    To read the lesson, and to learn the love,
To sound the depths of saddest chastisement,
    To pluck on earth the fruit of realms above.

Weep not too fondly, lest the cherished grief
    Should into vain, self-pitying weakness turn;
Weep not too long, but seek Divine relief;
    Weep not too fiercely, lest the fierceness burn.

Husband your tears; if lavished, they become
    Like waters that inundate and destroy;
For active, self-denying days leave room,
    So shall you sow in tears, and reap in joy.

It is not tears but teaching we should seek;
    The tears we need are genial as the shower;
They mould the being while they stain the cheek,
    Freshening the spirit into life and power.

Move on, and murmur not; a warrior thou—
    Is this a day for idle tears and sighs?
Buckle thine armour, grasp thy sword and bow,
    Fight the good fight of faith, and win the prize.

                        Rev. Horatius Bonar, D.D.

UNEXPRESSED.

DWELLS within the soul of every artist
   More than all his efforts can express;
And he knows the best remains unuttered,
   Sighing at what we call his success.

Vainly he may strive; he dare not tell us
   All the sacred mysteries of the skies:
Vainly he may strive; the deepest beauty
   Cannot be unveiled to mortal eyes.

And the more devoutly that he listens,
   And the holier message that is sent,
Still the more his soul must struggle vainly,
   Bowed beneath a noble discontent.

No great Thinker ever lived and taught you
   All the wonder that his soul received;
No true Painter ever set on canvas
   All the glorious vision he conceived;

No Musician ever held your spirit
   Charmed and bound in his melodious chains,
But be sure he heard, and strove to render,
   Feeble echoes of celestial strains.

No real Poet ever wove in numbers
    All his dream ; but the diviner part,
Hidden from all the world, spake to him only
    In the voiceless silence of his heart.

So with Love : for Love and Art united
    Are twin mysteries ; different, yet the same :
Poor indeed would be the love of any
    Who could find its full and perfect name.

Love may strive, but vain is the endeavour
    All its boundless riches to unfold ;
Still its tenderest, truest secret lingers,
    Ever in its deepest depths untold.

Things of Time have voices, speak and perish ;
    Art and Love speak, but their words must be
Like sighings of illimitable forests,
    And waves of an unfathomable sea.

                      ADELAIDE ANN PROCTER.

EASTER.

"Behold the place where they laid Him."—MARK xvi. 6.

SACRED sight! behold the place,—
  The sepulchre where Jesus lay!
    At either end an Angel sits
    In silent rapture, as befits
  The guardians of this wondrous day:
And in the midst that empty space.

Before one early streak of dawn
  Hath lit the Garden's hallowed shade,
    Lo, faithful women come to mourn,
    With costly spices duly borne,
  And eager hearts, yet sore afraid,
Whom holy love had thither drawn.

But what is this? From out the gloom
  Bright Angels tell their glorious news;—
    They show the swathings of the Dead,
    The napkin that was round His head:
  But over-blessèd hearts refuse
The tidings of the empty tomb.

Still week by week its Easter brings,—
   The holy day the Lord hath made:
     Yet, slow of heart, of spirit weak,
     We, trembling in the darkness, seek
   The Living One among the dead,
Though Death itself of glory sings.

But when the age has run its race,
   Behold, new-born from out the dust
     Ten thousand saints shall throng the air,
     And earth be left forsaken there;—
   The sleeping-place of all the just
An Easter-grave,—an empty space.

For now hath broke the Eternal Day;
   O wondrous morn of second birth!
     The blessèd dead in Christ arise
     To meet Him living in the skies:
   And they shall see new heavens,—new earth,—
No more the earth where Jesus lay!

                Rev. H. G. TOMKINS, M.A.

BREAD UPON THE WATERS.

"For now we see through a glass, darkly; but then face to face."—
1 Cor. xiii. 12.

SAY not, "'Twas all in vain,"
    The anguish, and the darkness, and the strife;
Love thrown upon the waters comes again
    In quenchless yearnings for a nobler life.
Think! In that midnight, on thy weary sight
    The stars shone forth—and 'neath their welcome rays,
Thine hopes to Heaven like birds first took their flight,
    And "thou shalt find them—after many days."

Say not, "'Twas all in vain,"
    The vigil, and the sickness, and the tears;
For in that Land "where there is no more pain,"
    The grain is garnered from those mournful years.
The faded form, once sheltered on thy breast,
    In gentle ministry thy care repays;
And smiling on thee from her sinless rest,
    Fear not to find her—"after many days."

Say not, " 'Twas all in vain,"
    Thy tenderness, thy meekness—oh! not so ;
A strength for others' sufferings shalt thou gain,
    As healing balms from bruisèd flowerets flow.
Weep not the wealth in fearless faith cast forth
    On the dark billows shipwrecked to thy gaze:
The bark was frail, the gem had still its worth,
    And "thou shalt find it—after many days."

Say not, " 'Twas all in vain,"
    The watching, and the waiting, and the prayer ;
In piercèd hands hath it unanswered lain ?
    'Twill grow more radiant as it lingereth there.
'Tis space—where once thy quivering form was cast,
    Thy heart-wrung sobs no floating breeze betrays ;
Yet, 'mid the white-winged choir thy prayer hath passed,
    And "thou shalt find it—after many days."

Say not, " 'Twas all in vain,"
    The patience, and the pity, and the word
In warning breathed 'mid passion's hurricane,
    Unheeded here—but God that whisper heard,
The tender grief, o'er strangers' sorrow shed,
    The sacrifice that won no human praise.
In faith upon the waters cast thy Bread,
    For "thou shalt find it—after many days."

ANNA SHIPTON.

"IN ALL TIME OF OUR TRIBULATION, GOOD LORD DELIVER US."

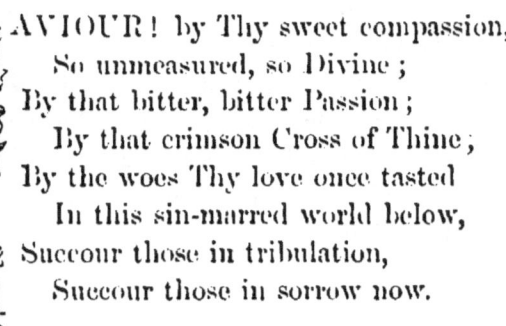

SAVIOUR! by Thy sweet compassion,
   So unmeasured, so Divine;
By that bitter, bitter Passion;
   By that crimson Cross of Thine;
By the woes Thy love once tasted
   In this sin-marred world below,
Succour those in tribulation,
   Succour those in sorrow now.

Thou Who wast so sorely burdened,
   Help the weak that are oppressed;
Sanctify all earthly crosses,
   For the coming day of rest;
Give the meek a trustful spirit
   That will always lean on Thee,
And in storms of deep affliction
   Still Thy gracious Presence see.

Lord, Thou hast a holy purpose
   In each suffering we bear;
In each throe of pain and terror,
   In each secret, silent tear;

In the weary days of sickness,
  Famine, want, and loneliness;
In our night-time of bereavement,
  In our soul's Lent-bitterness.

All the needful sweet correction
  Of this gentle Hand of Thine,
All Thy wise and careful nurture,
  All Thy faultless discipline;
All to purge the precious metal,
  Till it will reflect Thy face,
All to shape and polish jewels
  Thine own diadem to grace.

Lord, we know that we must ever
  Take our cross and follow Thee
All along the narrow pathway,
  If we would Thy glory see;
Then, O help us each to bear it,
  By Thine own hard life of shame,
Let us suffer well and meekly,
  Let us glorify Thy Name.

Cheer the weak ones who are bending
  'Neath this weary burden now;
Lift the pallid faces upward,
  Smooth the care-worn furrowed brow;
Send a bright and hopeful message
  To each tried and tempted heart,
That the thick and gloomy shadows
  At that sunshine may depart.

Tell them Thou canst see all sorrow
    In this world's rough wilderness;
Tell them Thou art near to succour,
    Near to comfort, and to bless:
Tell them of Thy Cross and Passion,
    Tell them of Thy trials sore,
Tell them of the Angel-city,
    Where is joy for evermore.

ADA CAMBRIDGE.

THE ISIS.

I LOVE the quiet river meads,
   Their memory is sweet to me,
For there were sown full many seeds
   Of what my life is yet to be.

I love the broad and grassy vale
   Where gentle Isis wanders slow,—
The horizon fringed with "poplars pale,"
   And where the willowy streamlets go;—

The antique bridge, the lofty spire
   Which tapers dark in golden air,
What time the slow-descending fire
   Of Summer eve is reddening there.

I love the foamy lasher-side,
   With dripping river-weed o'ergrown;
Where I would oftentimes abide,
   As silent as the mossy stone,

And watch the water, green and clear,
   To where it broke, and foamed, and flashed,
And lost itself in wild career,
   And to the pool with shouting dashed.

But most I love dear Isis' stream,
    Where, often in a lonely boat
I would not break the sunset gleam,
    But in the liquid lustre float,

And muse with inward sweet content
    On all the beauty round me there
In earth and sky together blent,
    A harmony most deep and fair,—

Or with a rapid stroke and strong
    Cleave through the water fresh and free,
Or, standing, slide the boat along,
    Like savage of the tropic sea;

Dipping an oar on either side,
    In narrow creek, or reedy pool,
Among the lily-leaves to glide,
    And in sequestered shadows cool,

Where floats the queen of river-flowers
    In loveliness of perfect grace,
Making through sultry Summer hours
    "A sunshine in a shady place:"

And where the groves of mellowed light
    Beneath the glassy water grow,
A dim-discerned, enchanting sight,
    Of green retirements deep below.

O happy river, golden hours,
    Of youth and health the choicest prime:
How throve the undistracted powers
    In life's most joyous morning-time!

When, after many years had passed
  With storm and sunshine o'er my head,
Once more my way was thither cast,
  And toward my native stream I sped,

Another heart, and yet the same,
  I felt; another life was mine:
But while I near and nearer came,
  The ancient light did clearer shine.

And musing as I paced along,
  When rose the lark with joyous cheer,
I thought he had another song,—
  The song my boyhood used to hear.

REV. H. G. TOMKINS, M.A.

WHEAT AND TARES.

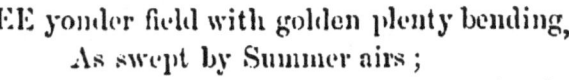

SEE yonder field with golden plenty bending,
    As swept by Summer airs;
Amongst the rustling ears, too closely blending,
    Are rank and wasteful tares!

Such is our life: our best and purest pleasures
    Are mixed with sad alloy;
And few among the soul's most cherished treasures
    But yield more grief than joy.

Even affections the most pure and holy—
    The spirit's choicest flowers—
Are intertwined with weeds of melancholy,
    And shade with gloom our bowers.

The holiest incense we present to Heaven
    Is mingled with strange fire!
The bread of life is blended with earth's leaven,
    Nor satisfies desire.

Ill dreams mix with our slumbers when reposing;
    Hopes are allied to fears;
Clouds blend with sunshine when the day is closing;
    Excess of joy brings tears.

A canker-worm round every gourd is creeping
　　That springeth from this earth;
The enemy sows tares while we are sleeping,
　　To mar our harvest-mirth.

Nought here is pure; all is confused and blended,—
　　The evil with the good;
The salvage of lost Eden has descended
　　With relics of the flood.

Yet will this mixture prompt no vain repining,
　　Nor the meek heart offend,
That might be asked, were all so bright and shining,
　　"How camest thou hither, friend?"

Here we expect not prizes, but probation;
　　Labour, and not repose;
Our safest triumph is some self-ovation,
　　And our best gifts our woes.

Patience awhile, the day of retribution
　　Will come, nor tarry long;
Each doubt will then receive a clear solution,
　　A remedy each wrong.

Let all grow on till harvest, tares still blending,
　　And dazzling the mocked eye;
The humbler corn, laden with worth, low bending,
　　In scorned humility.

The tares will then no more elude the reapers,
　　The fire will have its prey;
No enemy will mock the expectant sleepers,
　　Or steal their hopes away.

HENRY GODWIN, F.S.A.

THE DESIRED HAVEN.

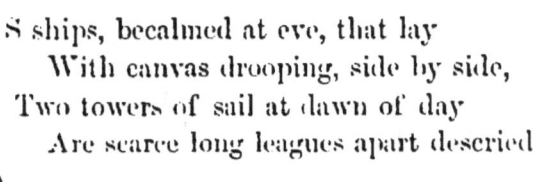

AS ships, becalmed at eve, that lay
   With canvas drooping, side by side,
Two towers of sail at dawn of day
   Are scarce long leagues apart descried;

When fell the night, up sprung the breeze,
   And all the darkling hours they plied;
Nor dreamt but each the selfsame seas
   By each was cleaving, side by side;

Even so—but why the fate reveal
   Of those, whom year by year unchanged,
Brief absence joined anew to feel,
   Astounded, soul from soul estranged.

At dead of night their sails were filled,
   And onward each rejoicing steered,—
Ah! neither blame, for neither willed,
   Or wist, what first with dawn appeared

To veer, how vain! On, onward strain,
   Brave bark! In light, in darkness too,
Through winds and tides one compass guides—
   To that, and your own selves, be true.

But, O blithe breeze ! and O great seas !
   Though ne'er, that earliest parting past,
On your wide plain they join again,
   Together lead them Home at last.

One port, methought, alike they sought,
   One purpose hold, where'er they fare,—
O bounding breeze ! O rushing seas !
   At last, at last, unite them there !

ARTHUR HUGH CLOUGH, M.A.

THE LIGHT OF THE WORLD.

PAINTED BY HOLMAN HUNT.

I.

> "Behold, I stand at the door, and knock: if any man hear My voice, and open the door, I will come in to him, and will sup with him, and he with Me."
> —REV. iii. 20.

IN the moonlight, when no murmur from
    the haunts of men is heard,
And the river in its sleep flows onward,
    onward to the sea,
And thou sleepest who art drawing nearer
    to Eternity,
    In the silence and the stillness comes
    the Word.

And He knocketh at thy portal, but thou
    dreamest in the night
That the flitting bat is only striking softly
    'gainst the door:
Shall He knock so oft who cometh from
    the Heaven's eternal Shore?
    Sleeper in the darkness, rise, behold thy
    Light!

'Tis thy Priest and Prophet, clad in jewelled robe and
   white attire;
'Tis thy King, and on His brow He wears the thorny
   coronal,
Budding now with amaranthine leaves and flowers am-
   brosial,
   In His face is speaking pity, silent ire.

For His glowing lamp discloseth, choking up thy dwelling
   door,
Deadly hemlock, barren darnel, prickly bramble, withered
   grasses,
And the ivy knits it closely to its stanchions, and passes
   Through the crevices, and hinges, and the floor.

Let Him in! for He will sojourn with the lowest and
   the least,
And forget that thou didst keep Him waiting in the
   dews and damp,
And for guerdon in the valley He will light thee with
   His lamp
   To the happy Shore Eternal, and the Marriage Feast.

B. A.,
Brasenose College, Oxford.

II.

Lord, Thou hast sought this wayward heart in vain;
   Choked by the world's vile weeds its portals stand,
   Closed to the touch of Thy redeeming hand,
Which, knocking gently, would an entrance gain:
Oh, Love unspeakable! that Thou shouldst be
   Patient amidst the night's chill falling dews,
   While I Thy proffered fellowship refuse,

Slothful to rise and ope the door to Thee :
Long have I tarried, dreading yet to bear
    The emblems of Thy suffering, thorns, and Cross ;
    Lost in idolatry of Mammon's dross,
And lured by pleasure's transitory glare :
Henceforth vouchsafe to shed Thy light within,
    Illume my soul, and let these contrite tears
    Blot out all record of my mis-spent years,
Dark with the sad remembrances of sin :
Then, in this purified repentant breast,
Enter! and be for evermore my Guest!

W. R. NEALE.

AUTUMN MEMORIES.

I.

BY THE LAKE.

HEMMED in by mountains, girdled with
    dark pines,
  The lake lay sleeping; not a ruffle
    stirred
Its deep, calm waters, and the lengthening
    lines
  Of shadow kissed its breast: no sound
    was heard.

Above, the clouds were coursing through the
    sky,
  Save where there gleamed a deep of
    purest blue;
And one star, like a signal lamp on high,
  Into a form of wondrous beauty grew.

It sparkled clear, like that strange star of
    old
  That led the wise men o'er their weary
    way,
Till they had brought their frankincense
    and gold,
  And worshipped where the world's Re-
    deemer lay.

I stood beside the margin; 'twas a sea
   Of glass; faint ripples dreamed along the shore:
I wondered if more beautiful could be
   The Land where seas and stars shall be no more.

And then I thought me of that lake of old
   Where once the Master 'mid the darkness trod,
And at His word the angry billows rolled
   Their foam into a calm, and owned their God.

Then o'er me came faint glimpses of a stream
   Whose waves make glad the City up above;
Lit up for ever by the sunny gleam,
   Reflecting only heavenly light and love.

Oh, when the storms of life have ceased to beat,
   Safe to the haven where we all would be,
Lord Jesu, bring our worn and wandering feet,
   Beside the margin of the Crystal Sea!

II.

IN THE CLOISTERS.

HARD by the lake, girt with its forest zone,
   The Abbey stands,—relic of days gone by:
The ivy clambers o'er the crumbling stone,
   And mosses sleep where the dead calmly lie.

Amid the ruins, o'er the chancel floor,
   The dank weeds thicken, and the rains descend;
The choir of voices sweet is heard no more,
   Nor to the altar priests their footsteps wend.

But memories cluster round the chapel grey,
    And, lingering there, we live the past again,
And seem to hear, adown the lonely way,
    The priestly footfall, and the solemn strain.

Still falls the yew-tree's shadow on the aisle,
    Wearing its crown of life amid decay;
Catching in early morn the sun's warm smile,
    Watching the stars gleam till the break of day.

Wait a few years, and that dark yew shall fade:
    But the true-hearted in their cloistered bed
Shall wake to life immortal, and, arrayed
    In robes of white, safe to their home be led.

That home, the Temple time can never dim;—
    No shadows frown, and no sad tears are there.
Oh, at the last, to join that ceaseless hymn,
    The crown of all His perfected to wear!

III.

AMONG THE RUINS.

A QUIET Autumn eve. The sun was flinging
    Long deepening shadows on the purple hill;
And, save the Vespers happy birds were singing,
    Or the faint sheep-bell, all was hushed and still.

The spot was sacred,—ruined arch and column,
    The traceried window, and the altar-stair,
Told of a worship, Catholic and solemn,
    That in the ages gone was offered there.

But now the porch, o'ergrown with weeds and grasses,
    Leads only to the crumbling aisle and nave ;
Along the groinèd roof the stray bat passes,
    While through the transepts winter tempests rave.

But 'mid the ruins, all unmarred and stately,
    A large stone Cross lifted its solemn head ;
The steps were worn, and the sight moved me greatly ;
    It seemed to speak of Life amongst the dead.

Emblem and shadow of a truth still deeper,—
    He who in Christ's dear Cross hath healing found,
Shall safe be garnered by the Angel Reaper,
    And stand secure upon the Holy Ground.

O Christ, the merciful High Priest and holy,
    Keep Thou these hearts from desolation free ;
And from their inner shrine, made pure and lowly,
    Let worship rise, like incense, up to Thee.

Cleanse them from earthly dross, Thou true Refiner,
    Thy living light upon their dimness pour ;
Until we see Thee in the Land Diviner,
    And with the Angels tread the Golden Floor.

IV.

AT SEA.

ROBED like a king, with coronet of gold,
    Grandly the sun went down beneath the sea,
Flushing the waves with amber as they rolled,
    And opening up the deeps of Heaven to me.

Around,—the waste of waters, the white foam
    Gathering in snowy flakes, and glittering spray;
Above,—the clouds, like great Cathedral dome,
    All tinted with the hues of dying day.

Yet this vast ocean, with its restless tides,
    He holdeth in the hollow of His hand;
The clouds, the chariot where His glory rides,
    And but His footstool all the peopled land!

Oh, Might and Majesty! all thought above,
    How eloquent these billows are of Thee!
O depth untold! O mystery of love,
    To know that outstretched Hand was pierced for me!

Rev. R. H. Baynes, M.A.

"THESE THREE."

O viewless angels by our side,
    With wings, but women sweet and good;
"These Three" indeed with us abide,
    True types of womanhood.
Yea, I, in turn, have reached a hand
    To each one of the blessèd Three:
In one fair group I've seen them stand,—
    Faith, Hope, and Charity.

My Faith hath misty hair,—and eyes,
    You cannot fix their changing hue;
But all the world within them lies,
    And all the soul looks through:
Her voice doth make Divinely sweet
    Each song of sorrow which she sings;
And saddest wisdom fills replete
    With heavenly comfortings.

My Hope is ruddy with the flush
    Of morning joy, that keeps its place
Though day has darkened, and the rush
    Of rain is on her face.

Her clear eyes look afar, as bent
  On shining futures gathering in ;
Nought seems too high for her intent,
  Too hard for her to win.

My Love hath eyes as blue and clear
  As clefts between the clouds of June,
A tender mouth, whose smiles are near
  To tears that gather soon.
Her best and loveliest she takes
  To light dark places ; wastes of life
She sows with precious seed, that makes
  All richest blessings rife.

Faith, when my soul in darkness dwells,
  Shall sing her song throughout the night ;
For each new effort life compels,
  Hope's clasp shall nerve with might ;
Love shall divide each grief of mine,
  Share every joy thus doubly given :
With each in turn life grows Divine,
  With all its tastes of Heaven.

ISA CRAIG.

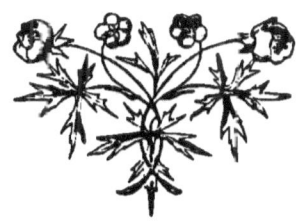

VISITATION OF THE SICK.

"Peace be to this house and to all that dwell in it!"

PEACE to this house!   O Thou Whose way
Was on the waves, Whose voice did stay
The wild wind's rage, come, Lord, and say,
   Peace to this house!

Thou, Who in pity for the weak
Didst quit Thy heavenly Throne to seek
And save the lost, come, Lord, and speak
   Peace to this house!

Thou, Who dost all our sorrows know,
And when our tears of anguish flow
Dost feel compassion, come, bestow
   Peace on this house!

Thou, Who in agony didst pray,
"Take, Father, take this cup away,"
And then wast strengthened, come and say,
   Peace to this house!

O Conqueror by suffering!
O mighty Victor! glorious King!
From out of pain and sorrow bring
   Peace to this house!

Thou, Who triumphant from the dead
Thine Hands didst o'er the Apostles spread,
And say, "Peace to you," come, and shed
    Peace on this house!

Thou, Who didst on the clouds ascend,
And then the Holy Spirit send,
Send Him to comfort and defend
    All in this house!

Lord, in the Sacramental food
Of Thine own Body and Thy Blood,
Peace that is felt, not understood,
    Give to this house!

Save, save us sinking in the deep,
Give ease from pain, and quiet sleep,
And under Thy wing's shelter keep
    All in this house!

"Peace to this house," come, Lord, and say;
Come to us, Lord, and with us stay;
O give, and never take away
    Peace from this house!

And when at last our fainting breath
On trembling lips scarce quivereth,
O bring us through the gate of Death,
    Lord, to Thine House!

To Thine own House in Paradise,
To Thine own House above the skies,
To live the life that never dies,
    Lord, in Thine House!

ARCHDEACON WORDSWORTH, D.D.

"HAVE MERCY ON ME, O LORD, THOU SON OF DAVID."

WITHIN the cool quadrangle's welcome shade,
  Beneath the linen awning, Jesus sought
A moment's quiet, while the fountain played
  Her pleasant interlude to weary thought.

Through the porch gleamed the rose-red sunset snows
  Of the wild crags of northern Galilee.
What awful life is in the God-repose
  That with the Past and Present welds Futurity!

Up the benched gateway thrills a woman's cry,
  As if the swollen torrent of deep care
Had torn down silence in its agony,
  To fling Grief's secret on the trembling air.

The loneliness of one unuttered woe,
  The silent tears when every hope had fled,
The sacred love, which mothers best may know,
  When sickness glooms around a firstborn's bed;

The weary hours beside her little child,
    The patient sadness of her darling's eye,
As with unselfish love she feebly smiled,—
    All, all came sobbing on that bitter cry.

O Lord, thou Son of David, pity me!
    So 'mid the wreck, bareheaded, 'gainst the spray
A drowning man might shriek across the sea,
    When hope of human help had passed away.

O Lord, thou Son of David, pity me!
    While ghastly doubt stung her sin-laden breast,
If for the guilt, done by her secretly,
    God's curse had fallen on what she loved the best.

He did not answer her one single word,
    Yet love was speaking in His every look:
When earth is silent, then may Heaven be heard,
    In sorrow's gloom Faith best reads God's own Book.

Think'st thou He hears not, when for many a day
    Thy knees are worn with fasting and with prayer?
Think'st thou He turns from any love away,
    Because thou seest no Angel on the air?

Tempter, away! each throb of pain He knows;
    I will kneel on, and wait His blessèd time:
Up the steep staircase of Life's darksome woes
    I'll climb and sing, till overhead God's Chime

Break with one roar of an eternal sea.
    And lo! if I have prayed He giveth more;
I stagger down, half blind with victory,
    Whispering the Chant from out the opening Door.

Rev. Alan Brodrick, M.A.

BY THE SHORE.

THE sun had set in glory; clouds of gold
   Were fringed with wondrous purple; crimson bars
Reddened the foaming billows as they rolled,
   Till from heaven's blue gleamed out the silent stars.

Then passed the Moon up to her queenly throne,
   The waters flashed with gems and glittering ore;
All earth was hushed to stillness, save the moan
   Of the monotonous waves along the shore.

I watched the strange clouds as they floated by,
   Some dark and murky, with a threatening glare;
Some white and fleecy mounting up the sky,
   Like veilèd angels on a shadowy stair.

And while I gazed I wondered what might be
    The new, diviner Land for which we wait;
For earth itself, from stain of evil free,
    Would gleam with glory from the Golden Gate.

But there no clouds shall gather, and no more
    The ocean rage—emblem of deep unrest;
No storms shall sweep across that radiant shore,
    No night shall shroud that City of the blest!

This earth is beautiful; o'er land and sea
    The mighty shadow of God's thought is cast;
But brighter far the Home that is to be,—
    O Christ! receive us to that Home at last!

Rev. R. H. Baynes, M.A.

JACOB'S LADDER.

AH! many a time we look on starlit nights
    Up to the sky, as Jacob did of old,
Look longing up to the eternal lights,
    To spell their lines of gold.

But never more, as to the Hebrew boy,
    Each on his way the Angels walk abroad,
And never more we hear, with awful joy,
    The audible voice of God.

Yet, to pure eyes the ladder still is set,
    And Angel visitants still come and go;
Many bright messengers are moving yet
    From the dark world below.

Thoughts, that are surely Faith's outspread-
    ing wings—
    Prayers of the Church, aye keeping time
    and tryst—
Heart-wishes, making bee-like murmurings,
    Their flower the Eucharist—

Spirits elect, through suffering rendered meet
    For those high mansions—from the nursery door
Bright babes that seem to climb with clay-cold feet,
    Up to the Golden Floor—

These are the messengers, for ever wending
    From earth to Heaven, that faith alone may scan ;
These are the Angels of our God, ascending
    Upon the Son of Man.

W. ALEXANDER, M.A.
Dean of Emly.

MOMENTS.

I LIE in a heavy trance,
   With a world of dream without me;
Shapes of shadow dance,
   In wavering bands, about me;
But at times, some mystic things
   Appear in this phantom lair,
That almost seem to me visitings
   Of Truth known elsewhere:
The world is wide,—these things are small;
They may be nothing, but they are All.

A prayer in an hour of pain,
   Begun in an under-tone,
Then lowered, as it would fain
   Be heard by the heart alone;
A throb when the soul is entered
   By a light that is lit above,
Where the God of Nature has centered
   The Beauty of Love:
The world is wide,—these things are small;
They may be nothing, but they are All.

A look that is telling a tale,
   Which looks alone dare tell,—
When a cheek is no longer pale,
   That has caught the glance, as it fell;

A touch, which seems to unlock
   Treasures unknown as yet,
And the bitter-sweet first shock,
   One can never forget:
The world is wide,—these things are small;
They may be nothing, but they are All.

A sense of an earnest will
   To help the lowly-living,
And a terrible heart-thrill,
   If you have no power of giving;
An arm of aid to the weak,
   A friendly hand to the friendless,
Kind words, so short to speak,
   But whose echo is endless:
The world is wide,—these things are small;
They may be nothing, but they are All.

The moment we think we have learnt
   The lore of the all-wise One,
By which we could stand unburnt,
   On the ridge of the seething sun:
The moment we grasp at the clue,
   Long-lost and strangely riven,
Which guides our soul to the True,
   And the Poet to Heaven:
The world is wide,—these things are small;
If they be nothing, what is there at all?

                      LORD HOUGHTON.

VOICE OF THE SEA.

WHAT means this tale, O Sea!
  Which thou hast told the earth since she was made?
A long and patient hearing hast thou had;
  And even yet thou wilt not let her be.

  The bare hills edged the strand,
Wherein was never sound of human speech,
When thy first breaker, falling on the beach,
  Began the tale we cannot understand.

  Thou hast seen tower, and hall,
And city, rise since then with tumult loud,—
And gather ivy round them for a shroud,—
  And sink into the silence waiting all.

  Trees have withstood thy breeze,
Which saw with thee how many a century passed;
Another ever rising o'er the last;—
  But thou hast seen the same befall the trees.

  The hills are scarred by man,
Though years passed o'er them, and could leave no trace;
But thou, each moment varying thy face,
  Art now the same as when the world began.

So long hath sounded here
Thy voice, O Sea ! repeating to the stones
One changeless tale, though said in many tones ;—
   Now half-subdued, as if in bashful fear,

   At urging it once more :
Now, when the Summer sunbeams on thee lie,
Thou seemest to repose, and lazily
   Murmur thy waves their message to the shore ;—

   Now passionate again,
They boom as if to storm Earth's reckless ear,—
Now sorrowful, because she will not hear,
   Sob forth all wearily the long refrain.

   And is the tale not done ?
Earth cannot comprehend ; her ear is chill.
Why art thou doomed to moan it round her still,
   E'en when she lies asleep beneath the moon ?

   Her lamps shine mutely down
Along thy foam ; her children sleeping lie ;
Above there bends the calm and silent sky ;
   Why shouldst thou only palpitate and moan ?

   The night will yet pass o'er,
The century close, upon thy murmur low.
What is it, then, which thou wouldst have us know ?
   The weight of treasures on thy sunless floor,

   Where no eye comes in quest ?
The lonely vastness of thine azure realm,
Where league-long waves each other overwhelm ?
   Or lieth so uneasy in thy breast,

All thou from earth hast ta'en?
Ah, Sea! too rich, indeed, are thy deep caves;
For, of the bright forms sunk beneath thy waves,
  Sun, moon, and stars are all that rise again!

    Yet—in that solemn chime,
Some holier secret surely hideth still.
Does yet thy voice with the remembrance thrill,
  Of that strange moment at the birth of time,

    When, 'midst thy primal sleep,
There came God's Spirit moving on thy breast,
And shook thee, trembling, from thy glassy rest,
  In quivering waves, which still pulsating keep?

    Ye two were all alone;
The embryo earth beneath lay dark and cold.
What wast thou in that wondrous contact told?
  What whispers didst thou hear of things unknown,

    Which filled the heart of God,
Before the first world on its axis turned?—
An infinite but lonely Love that yearned?—
  A purpose under all things lying broad?

    Ah, well thy tones may be
Mysterious! charged with meaning too profound
For thee to shape aright, or us to sound.
  Thou art but like the human soul, O Sea!

    When, with great thoughts oppressed,
Which the same Spirit through its voice would teach,
It can but hint them forth in broken speech,
  And seems to utter but its own unrest.

          AUTHOR OF "ANGEL VISITS."

ON THE THRESHOLD.

HOLD me not back, my children! Let me speed
   Onward, and ever onward; for the path
Which the great Master hath for me decreed,
    Its lines of glory hath!

The shadows fall behind me. See ye not
   That all is bright towards which my footsteps tend?
Come onward with me, towards the appointed spot,
    Which is my journey's end.

Come onward with me, towards the setting sun,—
   Towards the new morning portalled by the night,
When the allotted task of earth is done,
    And darkness merged in light.

See, through the opening vistas of the west,
   Bright glimpses of the Land toward which I am bound!
The crystal-wallèd City of the Blest,
    With Angel-watchers round.

On the Threshold.

Far mountain-ridges, gold and amethyst—
    Ascending spires of kingliest palaces;
And a calm ocean spread like sunlit mist,
    Betwixt myself and these.

And all as in a light of God doth shine;
    And on the margin of that sunlit shore
I see the loved, the young that once were mine,
    Not dead, but gone before.

And with their hands they beckon unto me,
    And with a voice-like melody they say,
"Here, O belovèd one, we wait for thee,
    Until thou pass away!

"Until thou pass away from earth and time—
    Till the night-shadows flee, and thou emerge
Into the fulness of the Day sublime,
    Of which thou seest the verge.

"Little remains to do as day grows late;
    Only to trust, to love with all thy heart,
To bless, like Christ the Lord; to stand and wait,
    And when He calls, depart!"

Thus speak the voices: O accept, my God,
    Thy servant's feeble sacrifice of praise,
For that Thy goodness has to me allowed
    The fulness of my days!

I praise and bless Thee! bless Thee for the gain
    Which, of Thy mercy, life has been to me—
Bless Thee for joy—bless Thee for grief and pain,
    Which brought me nearer Thee!

Lord, when Thou willest, call Thy servant hence;
    But, to the last, let love my being move;
Unto the last, like Thee, let me dispense
    From Thy great treasury, Love!

MARY HOWITT.

"SHE IS NOT DEAD, BUT SLEEPETH."

SHE rests in peace: beside her tomb
  The grasses wave, the low wind sighs;
Her spirit, in its "long, long Home,"
  Chants the glad music of the skies.
What matter, friends, though her dust sleep?
Her spirit lives; we will not weep.

Above her tomb the tall trees wave,
  The gentle shadows fall, and rest
In sorrowing on her silent grave
  Who leaneth on her Shepherd's breast.
What matter, friends, though her dust sleep?
Heaven took its own; we will not weep.

Amid the tears of our distress
  She passed to join the silent dead;
From sorrow and from weariness
  Her meek, long-suffering spirit fled.
What matter, friends, though her dust sleep?
Heaven took its own; we will not weep.

Beside the lowly house of prayer,
   Her tombstone, unto us forlorn,
Calming our grief, tells how from care
   She, in the solitary morn,
" Looking to Jesus," fell asleep.
God loves His own; we will not weep.

EDMUND SANDARS, B.A.

THE DYING SOLDIER'S WIFE.

H! well, the sun is sinking,—it will all be
over soon;
When the hungry jackals shriek to-night
to the yellow moon,
You will hear them, little daughter, and
shudder in your bed,
But I shall be gone, my darling, beyond
those bars of red.

For the sun is burning crimson, down on
the date-trees' crown,
And the hills in the distance rising show
purple, and blue, and brown;
Rising up height over height, sheer into
the hot thin air,
I can see them where I lie, like a tinted
marble stair,

Inlaid with green and amber, wrapt in a violet glow,
While the white pagodas shine, and the palm-trees shake
below:
But I would give all this glory for one pale northern
morn,
For the grey light in its heaven, and the gleam of its
golden corn.

It's far away in the West, and it's long ago, my dear,
But the shadows grow sharp and long, as evening draweth
    near;
And all the long day I have heard, across this sultry heat,
A patter of rain in the leaves, and the salt wave's tremu-
    lous beat.

It was early Autumn weather; the flax was in the pool,
And just this time of evening, but a night so calm and
    cool,
The curlew came up and cried in the shingle along the
    shore,
And the blue hills turned to black, as I stood at my
    father's door.

Ah! why should all this come back to-night on my dying
    brain?—
I heard their footsteps coming, and their voices in the
    lane.
Mother was in the byre; I, too, should have been there,
But I knew they were talking of me, and I slipped out
    unaware.

"Neighbour," my father was saying, "forty pounds has
    the lass,
And if you will not have her, you can even let her pass."
Washing, washing, washing, came the tide on the black
    rocks by,
But my heart beat louder and faster for fear of the man's
    reply.

He was the wealthiest farmer in all our country wide,—
But he was not to my mind, Jane, had he been an earl
    beside.

Angry and sharp came the answer,—" Forty is little," he
    said ;
" You should give your eldest daughter a trifle more to
    wed."

Spake out then your soldier father,—he stood the next to
    me ;
I knew it before he said a word, although I could not see :
" I reckon," said he, " there's that can never be bought or
    sold,
And if you give me Mary, I ask nor silver nor gold."

Washing, washing, washing, came the tide up over the
    stones,
Was it that or my own heart-beating that changed my
    Father's tones ?
" Forty pounds is her dower, and you shall have her,"
    said he.—
It's long ago, my darling, and it's far, far over the sea.

Ah ! why should all this come back to-night, when my
    brain is weak ?—
The rush of the wild south-wester, and the soft spray on
    my cheek,—
I've forgotten so many things, but this lives in my breast,
Like the blaze of a crimson dawn burnt into a gloomy
    west.

I've forgotten so many things, or they pass me by in a
    maze,—
The Sepoys' murderous battle, and Lucknow's weary days;

The dropping shot on the rampart, the sight of your
  Father's blood;
And the wail, and the fear, and the hunger, behind those
  walls of mud.

They pass me by like spectres, as I go down to the grave,
But a music tender and strange comes to me over the
  wave;
The church stands under the wood, where the hill dips
  to the loch,
She sings as a mother sings, when she makes the cradle
  rock.

Solemnly moves the pastor's lip, and as he prays and reads,
The words of love and of promise drop down like golden
  beads;—
Oh! it's well that strain has lingered within me to this
  day,
For it's little I've heard of Christ in this land where
  Christians sway.

Is it well, O land of glory! to send thy brave sons forth
From thy sunny southland meadows, thy grey cliff-
  guarded North?
You give them bread in the barracks, and weapons for
  the strife,
But not a Sword to fight the fiend, and not the Bread
  of Life.

From your valleys crowned with Churches, a dry Cross
  on their brow,
You send them out, with never a one to bid them keep
  their vow.

They fight your battles bravely; they die for you, sword
    in hand,
And leave their fair-faced orphans behind in a heathen
    land,—

Behind, with never a Church-bell rung, never a chanted
    psalm,
But hellish rite, and song impure, and the idol 'neath the
    palm.
They may grow up in that darkness; there's none to care
    or know—
O rich men over in England! O mothers! should this
    be so?

There's never a heart among you, up to the Queen on her
    throne,
But thrills when the terrible tale of this Indian War is
    known:
Never an eye but weeps, where her soldiers' arms are piled—
You give him tears and honour, give gold for his
    perishing child.

Hush! hush! they are passing away, the long wash of
    the sea;
And the singing down in the Church makes music no
    more for me:
I am drifting slowly homeward, and though there be
    clouds afar,
They touch but the sails of the ship that crosses the
    harbour bar.

For it's not the dying sun that shines in my dying eyes,
But a trail of the glory of Heaven over the mountain lies;

So lift me up, my darling, 'tis a gleam of the Golden
  Floor,
Through the Gate that is all one pearl, where Christ has
  passed before.

I have served Him badly, my child, weakly, below my
  desire,
Fearing, and falling, and rising, yet evermore coming
  nigher;
But as the sunbeam draws all other lights into its ray,
As the hand takes tenderly in the bird that wandered
  away,—

So the love of that Heart Divine absorbs my poor weak
  love,
So the Hand of my Saviour in Heaven takes in His weary
  dove;
And I could go so gladly, but ever there rises a mist—
'Tis you and your little sister—betwixt my soul and
  Christ.

CECIL FRANCES ALEXANDER.

GOING OUT AND COMING IN.

IN that home were joy and sorrow,
   Where an infant first drew breath,
While an aged sire was waiting
   Near unto the gate of death.
His feeble pulse was failing,
   And his eye was growing dim;
He was standing on the threshold
   When they brought the babe to him;

While to murmur forth a blessing
   On the little one he tried,
In his trembling arms he raised it
   Pressed it to his lips, and died.
An awful darkness resteth
   On the path they both begin,
Who thus meet upon the threshold,
   Going out and coming in.

Going out unto the triumph,
   Coming in unto the fight,—
Coming in unto the darkness,
   Going out unto the Light--
Although the shadow deepened
   In the moment of eclipse,
When he passed through the dread portal
   With a blessing on his lips.

And to him who bravely conquers
    As he conquered in the strife,
Life is but the way of dying—
    Death is but the gate of Life;
Yet awful darkness resteth
    On the path we all begin,
Where we meet upon the threshold,
    Going out and coming in.

DYING AMONG THE PINES.

DYING among the pines, the living pines,
    That hold their heads green all the Winter through,
And from their dark trunks, seamed with silver lines,
    Drop down all day their healing balm like dew,

Where the soft beat of the low pulsing sea
    Scarce ruffles on the level silver strand,
So well the pine woods, hanging on her lea,
    Filter the rough winds ere they touch the sand.

Dying, still dying,—far out in the wood,
    Over the sand, there lies a sacred ground,
Where quaint white wreath and roughly carven rood
    Tell that the toil-worn fishers rest have found,

Out in the wood, beyond the sandy reach
    Of the white domes. Ah me! 'tis far to lie!
There are no northern daisies by this beach;
    She had not need to come so far to die.

As when from some great ship in mid seas wrecked,
   A baby corpse is washed on some green isle;
For the short sleep that was so long bedecked
   In purest lawn, and wearing still a smile;

Which finding, the dark natives, with white teeth
   And plumèd heads, lay covered in a cave,—
So leave the English lady underneath
   The southern pines, beside the fisher's grave.

Through the green boughs aslant the warm sunbeams
   Shall wrap her feet as in a white lace shroud,—
Surely this wealth of natural life beseems
   Her better than the raindrop or the cloud.

What dim, faint gleams that symbol life unrols
   Of the great Life whereof the door is Death!
And that sweet love of Christ, that to our souls
   Is sun, and light, and shade, and balmy breath!

Dying among the pines: ah, lightly lie,
   White sand, that bearest nor violet, nor moss;
This earth is hallowed under every sky,
   A wreath of glory hangs on every cross.

CECIL FRANCES ALEXANDER.

"I HAVE THE KEYS OF HELL AND DEATH."

    LORD! Thine other names are sweet
      As music to the listening ear,
    But this thrills all our awe-struck heart
      With fitful pulse of gloomiest fear;
    Thou Lord of Heaven! and dost Thou dwell
    The holder of the keys of Hell?

    O Light of Love! O Fount of Life!
      Clear spring of joy for all on earth,
    Still quickening all to higher mood,
      Thou worker of the second birth;
    From Thee we draw each moment's breath,
    And art Thou, then, the Lord of Death?

Yea, Lord! through all that drear abyss,
    Where spirits wail their evil past,
Thy love and pity still look on,
    Long-suffering, conquering at the last:
From Thee flow mercy, pardon, peace,
From Thee the woe that shall not cease.

O Christ, eternal Light of Love!
    O Judge, eternal Fire of Wrath!
Guide Thou our steps the narrow way;
    Oh, lead us on the upward path:
Our darkness let Thy light illume,
Thy fire our baser dross consume.

We need not turn, for help or grace,
    To saints' or martyrs' pitying ruth,
For Thou art still the Way, the Life,
    In Thee all mercy meets all truth;
Oh, leave us not, Thou Lord of all,
Through pains of death from Thee to fall.

Oh, plunge us in Thy priceless blood!
    Oh, purge us in Thy cleansing fire!
Wash out each stain of sinful birth,
    Burn out each taint of low desire;
Through fire and water lead Thine own
To rest before Thy Father's throne.

Rev. E. H. Plumptre, M.A.

THE SONG OF THE BRIDE.

CALL all who love Thee, Lord, to Thee:
    Thou knowest how they long
To leave these broken lays, and aid
    In Heaven's unceasing song;
How they long, Lord, to go to Thee,
    And hail Thee with their eyes,—
Thee in Thy blessedness, and all
    The nations of the skies.

All who have loved Thee and done well,
    Of every age, creed, clime;
The host of saved ones from the ends
    And all the worlds of time:
The wise in matter and in mind,
    The soldier, sage, and priest,
King, prophet, hero, saint, and bard,
    The greatest soul and least;

The old, and young, and very babe,
    The maiden and the youth,
All re-born Angels of our age,—
    The age of Heaven and truth;
The rich, the poor, the good, the bad,
    Redeemed alike from sin;—
Lord! close the book of time, and let
    Eternity begin.

                  PHILIP JAMES BAILY.

AT THE ALTAR.

At the administration of the Lord's Supper on Whit-Sunday, my attention was attracted by the cries of a little child who had been left by his mother at her seat, while she waited with others at the altar. The boy struggled with those who tried to pacify him, and at last broke away from them and ran towards his parent, who was now kneeling at the rail. The child seemed to be awed by the solemnity of the scene, became unconsciously silent, and then knelt down by his mother's side. When I approached them with the consecrated bread and wine, he reached out his hand, as though supplicating for the spiritual food which I was offering to his mother.

This little incident suggested the following lines:—

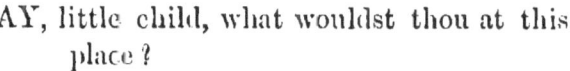

SAY, little child, what wouldst thou at this place?
  For kneeling at this sacred Fountain's brink
  Thou gazest silently, but must not drink.
What spell enthralls thee? Wouldst thou Christ embrace,
Ere yet thine infant feet have learnt to trace
  The thorny path which Christ's disciples tread?
  Or dost thou early feel thy spirit's need,
Thou youthful suppliant at the Source of Grace?
I know not. But I hail thy presence here,
  In token that thou wilt His servant be
    Hereafter, whom thou honourest now unknown,
And tearfully to Him I make my prayer,
  That He in mercy may remember thee,
    Thou little child, and mark thee for His own.

            VEN. ARCHDEACON BICKERSTETH, D.D.

THE DEATH OF DAVID.

[INSERTED BY SPECIAL PERMISSION OF THE PUBLISHERS, MESSRS. J. MASTERS AND CO.]

"So David slept with his fathers."—1 KINGS ii. 10.

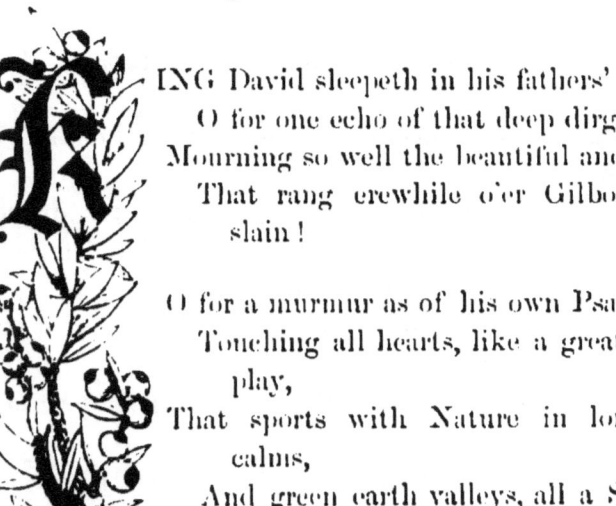

KING David sleepeth in his fathers' grave—
  O for one echo of that deep dirge-strain,
Mourning so well the beautiful and brave,
  That rang erewhile o'er Gilboa's royal slain!

O for a murmur as of his own Psalms,
  Touching all hearts, like a great wind at play,
That sports with Nature in long ocean calms,
  And green earth valleys, all a Summer's day!

From his calm face the shadows sharp and strong
  Of olden days have passed, and left it still;
From his closed lip the last low lingering song,
  Like the last echo flung back from a hill,

Has died away; and never, never more,
    So bold a hand shall sweep the silver lyre,
So true a tone shall teach to kneel and soar,
    So sweet a voice shall lead the saintly choir.

Warrior, and king, and minstrel more renowned
    Than ever touched fair fancy's noblest chord;
Saint with a wondrous weight of glory crowned,
    At once the type and prophet of his Lord;

He hath gone down into the shadowy vale—
    What though his face with many tears was wet,
Though sin's remorseful cry, though sorrow's wail,
    Swelled from that harp to heavenly music set;

Still in that grief we read a deeper sorrow,
    The awful mystery of a suffering God;
Still from that sharp, sin-laden cry we borrow
    A voice that mourns where our own feet have trod.

What though his warrior eye might ne'er behold
    On green Moriah's side the white stone flower,
For which his red right hand had piled the gold,
    Planning God's temple in his happier hour;

Still like a dream before his eye it slept,
    Its chambers flooded with a golden glow,
A strange bright place where faintest odours crept,
    From cedar-flowers eternally in blow.

And he had heard a grander music thrilling,
    Where needs no temple's marble wall to rise;
Had seen his glorious ritual's fulfilling,
    And known the One sufficient Sacrifice.

The Death of David.

As a great mountain on a stormy eve,
   After a stormy day, stands dimly shown,
—How many times we saw the grey mist weave
   A murky mantle for his crest of stone!—

Now a brief sunset splendour wraps his brow,
   A crimson glory on a field of gold,
Yet the wild tide is breaking dark below,
   Nor from its shaggy side the cloud has rolled—

So dim, so beautiful we see thy form,
   Conqueror and saint, man sinning and forgiven,
Around thee wrapt earth's shadows and its storm,
   With here and there a glimpse of purest Heaven.

But the morn breaks—a morning without clouds,
   A clear calm shining when the rain is o'er ;
He lieth where no mist of earth enshrouds,
   In God's great Sunlight wrapped for evermore.

Psalmist of Israel ! sure thou hearest now,
   If sweeter strains than thine can ever be,
A sweeter music where the elders bow,
   Striking their harps upon the Crystal Sea.

CECIL FRANCES ALEXANDER.

THE HOUR OF DEATH.

AY, wouldst thou die
When weeping clouds are in the sky,
When wind and rain
Beat fiercely on the window-pane,
And dark the tempest-drift goes by?

Or when the flowers
Are bright with sunshine and with showers;
When from their bloom
The fragrance rises to thy room,
And gladdens thee through lonely hours?

Or when the light
Is strong in Heaven? Or when the night
Hath veiled her face,
And hurries on with rapid pace,
Wouldst thou desire to pass from sight?

Or wouldst thou go
When Winter, with her shroud of snow,
Hath hid the ground,
Veiling in white each grass-grown mound?
Or when the golden lilies grow?

Say, wouldst thou be
Alone with Him Who calleth thee?
   Or wouldst thou have,
Within that shadow of the grave,
Kind faces round which thou mayst see?

   Nay, care not when
The messenger may come, if then
   He calls thee Home,
And with glad welcome bids thee come
Where mourners sorrow not again.

   Nor have one care
How Death may come to thee, or where,
   If only thou
Canst feel the light upon thy brow,
Beneath the Hand that does not spare.

   Dear Lord, with Thee,
Content with Thine all-wise decree,
   We leave the end;
For Thou, our Brother and our Friend,
Wilt one day come and make us free.

   Make us Thine own,
That we may know as we are known;
   Lord, make us Thine,
That we, within Thy Light Divine,
May see Thee crowned upon Thy Throne.

Rev. H. A. Rawes, M.A.

EMMAUS.

"ABIDE with us," they say, "the day is spent;
Abide with us, and rest." He set His Face
Towards the upland slope, where yet abide
The sentinels of twilight: still they urge
Redoubling their petition.
                            As He yields,
The board is spread: and at the frugal meal
They stand, and give God thanks; then sit and eat.
Nay! mark that Stranger now! He taketh bread,
He blesseth, and He breaketh.
                                And their eyes
Are opened, and they know Him!
                                      It is He,
The Lord of Whom they spake: the Lord that died,
And rose again, and lives for evermore.
And He hath vanished!
                          Oh to see Him yet!
"Did not our hearts burn in us as He showed
How Moses and the Prophets speak of Him,

His Death and Victory?"—That same hour they rise,
And, lighted by the Paschal Moon, that now
Floods holy Olivet with trembling light,
Wend back towards the city. There the Eleven
Had met this eve in silence and in fear,
With doors fast locked, lest enemies intrude.
Two days agone, "Though all men," was their boast,
"Reject Thee and deny Thee, yet not we:"
And they forsook the first!—And what if now
They who forgat Him be by Him forgot?
What if the golden chain of love be snapped?—
Nay, never, never deem it! This His law:
Loving His own, He loves them to the end.
Meanwhile, up hill, through copse, down vale, they go,
Where lately He was with them: on they press,
With this one yearning hope, to tell the tale
That shall remove all fear and end all doubts.
Now they have reached the portal; now they meet
The challenge of the soldier: now they tread
The dim and silent city streets, and gain
The upper room, that kernel of the Church.
And lo! they hear the tale they thought to tell:
"The Lord is risen indeed, and hath appeared
To Simon!"
    O the joy of joys! O Day
Blest beyond all days! Portal to the sky!
The golden ladder, lifting man to God!
And Thou,—what tongue can tell Thy praise?— what
 heart,
Bursting in thankfulness, can sing Thy love,
Thou vanquished Victor, Crucified Supreme,
That reignest, because Thou sufferedst? Thou hast now

Done with those woes for ever: Thou hast left
That glorious Τετέλεσται to Thy band
Battling in this world; Thou upon the vault
Of "terrible crystal,"* which the Angels tread,
Standest in the midst, the Lamb that hast been slain;
And seest the prostrate Elders, and the Four
Mysterious Living Creatures, and the souls
Perfect through suffering, that have reached Thy Land
By the same path Thou troddest; and how they strike
Their purest light-harps, and ascribe to Thee
The glory, and the wisdom, and the might,
The victory and salvation!
     Grant me, God,
One day, the lowest place beneath their feet!

Rev. J. M. Neale, D.D.

* Ezekiel i. 22.

London: J. & W. Rider, 14, Bartholomew Close.

TWENTY-FOURTH THOUSAND.

Handsomely printed on toned paper, extra cloth, antique, 3s. 6d.

Lyra Anglicana

HYMNS AND SACRED SONGS

COLLECTED AND ARRANGED

BY THE

REV. R. H. BAYNES, M.A.

Of St. Edmund Hall, Oxford.

"A more elegant little volume in appearance, and one more calculated to meet with a hearty reception from all to whom sacred songs are dear, has not for a long time issued from the press. The Hymns are at once devout and beautiful."—*Press.*

"In all respects a devotional book, and cannot fail to meet many sincere admirers."—*Liverpool Albion.*

"Most of the pieces have a more finished poetical character than the generality of Hymns."—*Clerical Journal.*

"A beautiful edition of Hymns and Sacred Songs. Among the pieces are several exquisite gems."—*Newcastle Guardian.*

"If we have not quoted enough to send the reader to the volume, we should add extract to extract in vain."—*Newcastle Daily Chronicle.*

"Its intrinsic merits are very considerable."—*Spectator.*

"Both the character and object of the work warmly recommend it to favour."—*Edinburgh Evening Courant.*

"Deserves warm recommendation."—*Guardian.*

"The printer, the paper-maker, and the binder have united their skill to give a finished beauty to the book, which we have great pleasure in heartily recommending."—*Literary Churchman.*

"A choice selection of Sacred Lyrics, worthy of being placed in every Christian's library. Beautifully printed on fine paper, and elegantly and substantially bound, the volume is well adapted for a present to a Christian friend."—*City Press.*

"One of the cheapest Christmas present books out. It is capitally got up in the antique style, as regards type, paper, and binding; and the contents are generally good."—*Brighton Herald.*

HOULSTON & WRIGHT, 65, PATERNOSTER ROW, LONDON.

Cloth, sprinkled edges, ONE SHILLING; fine edition, toned paper; cloth, red edges, EIGHTEENPENCE.

THE
Canterbury Hymnal

A BOOK OF COMMON PRAISE

ADAPTED TO

THE SERVICES IN THE BOOK OF COMMON PRAYER

SELECTED AND ARRANGED

BY THE

REV. R. H. BAYNES, M.A.

Editor of "Lyra Anglicana."

"Selected with great care, and framed in close accordance with the spirit and temper of the Services, and adapted to the successive Seasons of the Church. We could heartily wish that a Hymn Book such as this could be selected by the Archbishop of Canterbury."—*Press.*

"None but those who are engaged in it know what are the difficulties in compiling such a book, and the thanks of Churchmen are due to Mr. Baynes for his arduous labours."—*John Bull.*

"Seems fully to have accomplished all it aims at. It is better as poetry, more catholic in spirit, and more genial in tone, than any other Hymnal we are acquainted with."—*South-Eastern Gazette.*

"Well selected and thoroughly orthodox are the Hymns brought together in this chastely got-up congregational Hymnal."—*Dover Chronicle.*

"Printed in excellent clear type, and peculiarly pretty yellow-tinted paper."—*Reader.*

HOULSTON & WRIGHT, 65, PATERNOSTER ROW, LONDON.

www.ingramcontent.com/pod-product-compliance
Lightning Source LLC
Chambersburg PA
CBHW031750230426
43669CB00007B/560